ISBN 978-0-243-23593-3
PIBN 10789907

This book is a reproduction of an important historical work. Forgotten Books uses state-of-the-art technology to digitally reconstruct the work, preserving the original format whilst repairing imperfections present in the aged copy. In rare cases, an imperfection in the original, such as a blemish or missing page, may be replicated in our edition. We do, however, repair the vast majority of imperfections successfully; any imperfections that remain are intentionally left to preserve the state of such historical works.

Forgotten Books is a registered trademark of FB &c Ltd.
Copyright © 2018 FB &c Ltd.
FB &c Ltd, Dalton House, 60 Windsor Avenue, London, SW19 2RR.
Company number 08720141. Registered in England and Wales.

For support please visit www.forgottenbooks.com

1 MONTH OF
FREE
READING

at
www.ForgottenBooks.com

By purchasing this book you are eligible for one month membership to ForgottenBooks.com, giving you unlimited access to our entire collection of over 1,000,000 titles via our web site and mobile apps.

To claim your free month visit: www.forgottenbooks.com/free789907

* Offer is valid for 45 days from date of purchase. Terms and conditions apply.

English
Français
Deutsche
Italiano
Español
Português

www.forgottenbooks.com

Mythology Photography **Fiction** Fishing Christianity **Art** Cooking Essays Buddhism Freemasonry Medicine **Biology** Music **Ancient Egypt** Evolution Carpentry Physics Dance Geology **Mathematics** Fitness Shakespeare **Folklore** Yoga Marketing **Confidence** Immortality Biographies Poetry **Psychology** Witchcraft Electronics Chemistry History **Law** Accounting **Philosophy** Anthropology Alchemy Drama Quantum Mechanics Atheism Sexual Health **Ancient History** **Entrepreneurship** Languages Sport Paleontology Needlework Islam **Metaphysics** Investment Archaeology Parenting Statistics Criminology **Motivational**

VALENTINO
AS I KNEW HIM

By S. GEORGE ULLMAN

With an Introduction
By O. O. McINTYRE

A. L. BURT COMPANY
Publishers   New York

Published by arrangement with Macy-Masius

Printed in U. S. A.

"VALENTINO AS I KNEW HIM"
IS COPYRIGHT, 1926, BY
MACY-MASIUS: PUBLISHERS

Published October, 1926
Third printing, March, 1927

MADE IN THE UNITED STATES OF AMERICA

WITH DEEP APPRECIATION TO
LILIAN BELL
AND
RAYMOND FAGER

An Introduction to This Book
by O. O. McIntyre

I was one of those who confused Rudolph Valentino with the vaselined dancing world of Broadway's meandering mile, until I met him. I was not alone. Many did this while Valentino, frightened and questioning, swept on until he became the most amazing figure of our time.

Valentino was never sure of himself. True genius never is. He was constantly lifting his eyes to the hills. I have sat with him in the curtained box of a theater while first showing of his films evoked laughter and tears; and always he sat motionless, moist-eyed and pale.

No man I have ever known was quite so humble in success. It is trite for the artist to say he wants to do better things. Valentino would never say it, but he felt it to the very depths.

Next to George Ullman, I suppose I shared as many of his serious confidences as any man. He came to me many times, perplexed, harassed and soul-spent—but never defeated. His courage was boundless.

Introduction

During those dark days when he broke off relations with the Famous Players and dropped like a plummet from the movie pinnacles to the semi-obscurity of "barnstorming", I ran across him in Chicago. His future was uncertain and already there were murmurings of a fickle public: "Valentino is through!" . . . adrift on the shoreless sea.

He was never gayer, for responsibility crushed him, and he had cast off the fetters. "When I pay off my debts barnstorming," he said joyously, "I am going to live"; and he was like an eagle poised for flight.

No apologia is needed for Rudolph Valentino, despite the fact I doubt if ever a man in the public eye was so misunderstood. He became involved in that senseless abracadabra that singled him out as "a sheik"—and how he despised that appellation!

He once attended a little dinner party of mine at which Meredith Nicholson, the distinguished Indiana novelist, was the guest of honor. In recounting the list of guests to Nicholson before the dinner I mentioned Valentino. He said nothing, but I could see he was rather surprised.

And yet, five days after Valentino's passing came this note from that kindly and learned man: "Poor Valentino! I could not reconcile the press

by O. O. McIntyre

agent stuff about him with the lad himself after meeting him at your party. He was splendid."

Valentino impressed himself in that manner upon every one with whom he came in contact. He was always appealingly shy, but when he spoke you listened, for his words were surcharged with an eager vitality. He was a scholar, indeed a poet; and had he used his pen as an Alpine stock he would have scaled the Matterhorn.

But he was not always the dreamer knocking his head against the stars. His vision was more practical than not, as is shown by his "come back" when the betting was 100 to 1 in astute cinema circles that he wouldn't.

He had an extremely human side which was displayed in his appreciation of the ridiculous. He often plagued me about my propensity for loud clothes. From here and there he would send me ties that hooked and snapped on, the color of poisonous wall paper.

Once, when we talked on the telephone, I said: "Drop around, I have a new tie." An hour later, on this warm summer day, he came in gravely wearing fur ear-muffs as though to muffle the din.

Another time, from Spain, he sent me a postcard of himself taken with a goat. A slight imperial graced Valentino's chin. He wrote: "The one with whiskers is the goat."

Introduction

Still another time he said to me: "It sometimes worries me that you might think that, because I invite you to the first showing of my films with me, I am seeking a little publicity through the things you write. It would please me if you would never mention me in any of your articles. I would like to think our friendship transcends that." He was tremendously sincere and, until he died, I never mentioned him after that until his passing.

Valentino was particularly abstemious as to liquor. He had been reared in a land where a goblet of wine was an essential with meals, and this he enjoyed; but that was all. He smoked innumerable cigarettes, but his was a strong physique and, outside of smoking, he took excellent care of himself.

He was totally and sincerely oblivious to the gaping of the curious. Mrs. McIntyre and I once stepped out of his automobile in front of our hotel after a drive with him and Natacha Rambova. He preceded us and stood to chat for a few moments. The sidewalk soon overflowed with curious. He suddenly saw them and exclaimed: "I think something has happened in your hotel." He did not realize until a few seconds later he was the object of the attention. Then he sheepishly lifted his hat, blushed and rode away.

By O. O. McIntyre

One night in St. Louis, when he was making personal appearances, I happened to be in the city. A mutual friend invited us to dinner at a pleasure resort on the outskirts. Downstairs some factory employees were giving a dinner to relieve the tedium of rather hum-drum lives. It became noised about that Valentino was upstairs.

Timid faces began shyly to peep in the door to gaze at Valentino. A message finally came up that these workers would like to see him. He was touched. "Why, I'll dance for them!" he said, and he went down and, looking over the crowd, selected, I am sure, the most poorly dressed girl in the gathering, bowed to her in the courtly manner of a true gallant, and swung off into a waltz.

Valentino loved the author of this book in the manner of a devoted brother. He did nothing of importance without "discussing it with George". And no one was so grievously stricken by his passing as Ullman. It was a heart-wrench that will be with him always.

I last saw Valentino in Paris, a few months before he died. He called on me at the apartment in which I was living on Avenue Henri Martin. Gray dusk was sifting through the delightful pink of Paris twilight. We went for a walk out beyond the Trocadero and sat on a bench. In the distance

Introduction

Eiffel Tower was scissoring its network of starry squares against the plush of night. We talked of many things; I do not recall them now, but I do remember walking on later to the Arc de Triomphe, where I bade him good-by and saw him swing down the brilliantly-lighted Champs Elysée, his head held high.

And it has pleased me that Valentino justified my faith in him in that adventure called death just as he had in the adventure of life. Not once did he falter. Not even in that black moment when, ghastly pale and weak, he said to his doctor, with a wan smile, "Doctor, I guess we won't go on that fishing trip after all."

So he turned his face to the wall and his indomitable spirit burst from dull clay, free.

And as I write these concluding lines to my friend, I think of those far worthier lines of Edna St. Vincent Millay:

> My candle burns at both ends;
>   It will not last the night;
> But ah, my foes, and oh, my friends—
>   It gives a lovely light!

Valentino as I Knew Him

Chapter 1

WITH the death of Rudolph Valentino, at the very height of his career, came a demand from the public for an intimate story of his life.

In attempting to construct such a story, I am confronted by the problem of sifting chaff from wheat, of separating those colorful stories in newspapers and magazines from the real Valentino, who was known only to his intimates.

Life seldom flows smoothly for any man; but, concerning one who from his earliest youth experienced vicissitudes such as fall to the lot of few, the telling of them becomes a task not to be lightly attempted.

I gather my material, for this last tribute to my friend, from stories he told me here and there, some related in the great bay window of his Hollywood home, some on horseback riding over the desert at Palm Springs, some on our long railway journeys between California and the East.

In writing these memoirs, I can only hope that, in my desire to place a true image of my beloved friend before the public, I have not too intimately delved into the recesses of his private life, or bared

Valentino as I Knew Him

secrets of his soul which he, naturally reticent, would have resented.

His whole name was Rodolpho Alfonzo Raffaelo Pierre Filibert Guglielmi di Valentina d'Antonguolla, a big handicap for a helpless child. No matter how poor Italians may be in money, the poorest is rich in adjectives, gestures and names.

When Rudy came to this country he found that no one would listen to him long enough for him to tell the whole of his name. This is a busy country; every one is in a hurry.

Being told frequently to snap out of it and cut it short, Rudy was confronted with the necessity of selecting that part of his name which would best bear translation into Americanese.

He therefore selected Rodolpho Valentino, and at first was insistent on this spelling of his name. But the public insisted upon spelling it Rudolph and pronouncing it Rudolph, so that finally he submitted, and adopted the name Rudolph Valentino as his own.

Now, in telling the story of his life, I find that I cannot relate it in proper sequence. I cannot begin with his birth and go historically on through the changing scenes to his tragic and untimely death.

I must sometimes start with an incident in his childhood and skip to the effect this had upon his

Because his most distinctive success was as Julio in The Four Horsemen, this was one of his favorite pictures

by S. George Ullman

later life. Or I must go back, from the years in which I knew him, to the days of his early struggles in New York, long before he and I became friends.

Nor will I attempt to go deeply into that part of his life which was devoted to hard work, to the making of his pictures. Nor will I touch upon that side of him which the public already knows or can imagine.

At the risk of imputing to him the life of a butterfly, a lover or a man interested solely with the glamorous side of life, I shall tell what I knew of him, from long intimate talks in which he, realizing that I was sympathetic, would expound his theories of life, his philosophy, his dreams and ambitions.

If it is true that mixed strains of blood produce the unusual, then Valentino's ancestry is partly responsible for his genius. His mother was a French woman, the daughter of a Paris surgeon, Pierre Filibert Barbin. His father, Giovanni Guglielmi, was a Captain in the Italian cavalry.

In her early life, his mother experienced the terrors of the siege of Paris. After she had married his father, the Guglielmi family settled in the little town of Castellaneta, in the southernmost part of Italy.

With flashing eyes, and enacting the scenes

Valentino as I Knew Him

which led to the driving of his ancestors thus southward, Rudy told me how it came about.

One ancestor was a brave fellow, according to the story, which undoubtedly grew more picturesque as it passed down the generations. He had the misfortune to get into a quarrel with a member of the Colonna family, one of the finest and oldest in Rome.

As is generally the case in Italian quarrels, it was a matter of caste, a Romeo and Juliet affair. Guglielmi killed the Colonna and was forced to flee from Rome. The men who supported Guglielmi in his quarrel fled into exile with him. They were forced to masquerade as shepherds, and finally settled among the peasants in the province of Leece.

While describing this duel, which doubtless took place on foot, Rudy was on horseback. Thereupon he turned the story into a duel on horseback, so realistic that I asked him if this duel took place in the time of the Crusades! This brought Rudy to, possibly just in time to save my life, as, for the moment, he seemed to imagine that I was the Colonna. But I had no wish to return from an innocent ride on a stretcher.

Brought back to his narrative, he said that in 1850, when Ferdinand di Bourbon ruled over Naples and Sicily, brigands stormed the little

by S. George Ullman

town of Martini Franco, where the Guglielmi had settled. In the massacre which ensued, the family were again forced to flee, and this time they settled in Castellaneta, bringing with them only the clothing they wore.

"Ours was a typical farm house," he told me, "built of heavy white stone, flat roofed and square, with its thick walls interspersed by casement windows, whose heavy blinds were barred at night. On the main floor was the large living room, dining room, kitchen and my father's study. About a courtyard in the rear were the servants' quarters and stable."

We dismounted and with a stick he drew in the sand the ground plan of this house.

With his arm through the bridle of his horse, standing on the desert sands in the white California moonlight, Rudy harked back to certain things which he remembered. He was a gallant figure, handsome as a centaur, and I could see that he was intensely proud of these early impressions.

"Take my names," he said. "My mother explained very carefully how I came by each of them. You Americans make fun of them, because they are so many, but they were a matter of grave import to her. To my father's house belong the Rodolpho Alfonso Raffaelo. The Pierre Filibert, I inherited from her father. The di Valentina

Valentino as I Knew Him

was a papal title, while the d'Antonguolla indicates an obscure right to certain royal property which is now entirely forgotten, because that wretched ancestor of mine fought a duel with the great house of Colonna and so offended them.

"My father died when I was but eleven. He called my older brother, Alberto, and me to his bedside, and said: 'My boys, love your mother and above all love your Country!' Even on his death-bed he was true to his calling, a Captain of cavalry.

"I remember the funeral, too. It was military. There was a coach drawn by six horses, the coachmen wearing a uniform of black and silver, my father's four dearest friends walking beside the hearse, and holding the four large tassels which depended from it. And, in the carriage with my mother, we three children rode, awed by her grief, and hardly knowing what it was all about."

Rudy was then sent to the Dante Alighieri College, which corresponds to one of our grammar schools. He remained here two years and then was sent to a military academy.

One of the greatest mistakes in the world is to ignore the inner life of a talented child. The fact that young Valentino was a dunce at school, badly behaved and impossible of control, should

by S. George Ullman

have been warning to his mother that his mind would bear investigating.

While apparently poring over books, in reality the child was a million miles away: a hero, a bandit, a gypsy, a toreador, or a Rajah. He was even then laying the foundation of his ability to enact romantic characters. I have no doubt that he was often cuffed on the ear or switched back to every-day life, from an imaginary gallop over the desert at the head of his faithful band of retainers. Indeed he told me that the books of adventure he read during these troublous periods, in which he attempted to absorb a knowledge of books, were the real beginnings of his ability to act, because he understood his rôles from the inside.

When will the time come, I wonder, when educators will attempt to understand unruly children and utilize their impulses toward their chosen work, instead of beating or expelling them!

The reason for which Rudolph Valentino was expelled from the Dante Alighieri College was the very reason for which, thirteen years later, he was able to play *Julio* in *The Four Horsemen of the Apocalypse.*

The King, the great King Vittorio Emanuele, husband of the lovely Queen Elena, was to pass by. And poor Rudy, stripped to his underclothes

Valentino as I Knew Him

for a misdemeanor, was left in the dormitory as a punishment.

Knowing where his clothes were concealed, Rudy broke into the locker, dressed and dashed madly down the deserted streets, to find the crowd which marked the King's progress. From a coign of vantage, high above the heads of the people, he watched the procession, the King on his coal-black charger passing so close that the boy was almost able to reach out his hand to touch him. The good children of the school, herded by a professor, were in a position from which they could not see nearly so much as the disobedient adventurer, who, the next day was ignominiously packed home as a punishment.

What did it matter? He had seen the King! And furthermore, in the dormitory that night, with sheets for his uniform, he enacted for the good children what his close-up of the King had really signified, embellishing it, no doubt, with details from his own fervid imagination at which the good King would have gasped had he been able to hear.

Thus, in a blaze of glory, the sinner fared forth from the Aleghieri College; in the minds of the students, going forth to conquer the world.

His mother did not share this enthusiasm.

Determined to educate this incorrigible, she

by S. George Ullman

packed him off to a military academy at Perugia. This was the Collegio della Sapienze, destined for the sons of physicians.

The military atmosphere of this school fired Rudy's youthful imagination. He decided to become a cavalry officer. This is quite excusable, as most of the officers in the Italian cavalry come from noble families, and are the flower of the land. Also, they wear one of the most beautiful uniforms in the world. The women, particularly, admire the long, glorious blue cape of this uniform.

But when Rudy divulged this ambition to his mother, she explained to him the great expense this career entailed and told him that, while his father had left a comfortable little fortune, it was not sufficient to enable him to realize this ambition.

Being enough of a man to realize this, Rudy compromised on the Royal Naval Academy, in preparation for which the youth seemed to settle down to real study for the first time in his life. For the physical examination, he trained strenuously and got himself into physical trim, doubtless laying the foundation for that physique which was the marvel of every one when he came into pictures.

When, however, the fateful day arrived for

Valentino as I Knew Him

his physical examination, candidate Guglielmi was found to be lacking an inch in chest expansion. After his efforts to achieve the perfection necessary, this deficiency was the most humiliating thing which had ever come to him.

And now was brought out one of the salient characteristics of Valentino. He never could accept defeat. When confronted with such a shortcoming as this, nothing in life was so important as that he should correct it then and there. There was no putting it off to a future time, slurring it over with a shrug or an "Oh, never mind! I'll do better next time." No. On that very instant the work must be begun, to give him a chest expansion which would *more* than fulfill the requirements of any naval academy on the top of the round earth.

This humiliation was like the flick of a whip on the back of a spirited horse. Rudy, of his own accord and with no one to force him, put himself into such marvelous physical shape that never, to the day of his death, did he lose any part of it.

Nevertheless, this failure to enter the Royal Naval Academy marked another milestone in the life of the boy. He was but fifteen yet, in his wounded pride he felt that life was over, that his mother would be forever ashamed of him, and

by S. George Ullman

that the best thing he could do would be to end his life.

With a woman's intuition, his mother sensed this, for she took the boy into her arms, assuring him that she never wanted him to be in the Navy anyway, that it was too dangerous a profession and that in her secret heart she was glad that he had not been accepted.

"Better far," said she, "that you go to the Royal Academy of Agriculture and study the science of farming. Italy has need of scientific farmers far more than she has of soldiers and sailors."

Had not his most distinguished ancestors proudly tilled the soil of their estates? Might not he, her son, become a great landed proprietor and recreate the glories of the family?

At these inspiring suggestions, the head of young Valentino went up and again his ambition flamed.

Once more he started forth to school, this time with a high and lofty purpose, and it was with great satisfaction that he finally graduated with the highest honors in his class, showing that he could have succeeded earlier if he had put his mind to it. But he was too full of Romance.

This success seemed to go to his head, for nothing would now do but that he must go to Paris to conquer that metropolis. At first, since he had

Valentino as I Knew Him

some money, he was quite successful, for youth and manly good looks he found to be at a premium.

As soon, however, as his money was gone, he found things vastly different and, in a panic, he sent home for more funds. When these came, they were found to be such a modest amount that it would not go far.

Therefore, accepting the advice of the friends he had made in Paris, he rushed off to Monte Carlo to increase his fortunes by gaming. With the usual result.

Penniless, mortified and humiliated, he sat down to take a mental account of stock.

"Certainly I had done nothing to win the title of 'Pride of the Family,'" he told me. "The honors I had achieved at the Agricultural Academy had been entirely wiped out by my escapades in Paris and Monte Carlo. What to do I did not know. The family, including my uncle, who had taken care of my father's estate, met in solemn conclave. They discussed me pro and con, and their conclusions were not flattering. Their decision was to ship me to America. 'For,' said my uncle, 'if he is going to turn out to be a criminal, it is better for him to be in far off America where his disgrace can not touch us.'"

We both looked at each other and laughed as he repeated these gloomy predictions. George

by S. George Ullman

Eliot speaks somewhere of "the brutal candor of a near relation." And certainly Valentino had received an example of this.

"I wonder what would have become of me," he said, "if I had stayed in Castellaneta, bought a piece of land and become a scientific farmer? Can you picture the scene?"

He was wearing the costume of *The Son of the Sheik* when we had this talk, so that his question needed no answer.

With the prospect of America near at hand, his mother raised a sum of money, more possibly than she could afford, and sent him to America on the Hamburg-American liner *Cleveland,* which arrived in New York two days before Christmas, 1913.

Chapter 2

Young Valentino, when he set sail, knew not a single word of English; on the way over, he made every effort to pick up a few words. As they sailed into the harbor and he caught his first view of the New York sky line, he asked a young Italian friend where to go when he landed, and was told of an Italian place, Giolitto's, in West 49th Street.

The gay life in Paris, along with its many disasters, had taught Rudy the one thing which he now found needful, and that was to dance. From some South American friends of his he had learned the tango, so that, when his money gave out in America, and he had tried many forms of work, failing gloriously in most of them, his thoughts turned to the one thing he could do well, namely, dance.

With this in mind, he applied first to the manager of a restaurant where he had formerly appeared as a guest. Here he did so well that it was not long before one of his admirers mentioned him to Bonnie Glass, and brought about an introduction.

She was then in need of a dancing partner to

Valentino as I Knew Him

take the place of Clifton Webb. She invited Rudy to her hotel the next afternoon and, after the first try-out, Miss Glass engaged him at a salary of fifty dollars per week. To him this salary seemed enormous and nothing short of a god send. With Bonnie Glass as a partner, Valentino's dancing soon took on distinction and the sucecss these two achieved put confidence into a heart which had more than once begun to fail him, causing him to wonder if indeed he had done right to leave his own country.

While Valentino never aspired to be a dancer in the class of Mordkin, yet no one who had ever seen him dance the tango with a suitable partner could ever forget it. He was not dancing the tango, he was the tango. His was the drama of the dance.

His partnership with Bonnie Glass was very fortunate. They danced at the Winter Garden, the Colonial, the Orpheum in Brooklyn, many Keith houses, and even went on tour. In Washington President Wilson attended their opening and they received sixteen curtain calls for a waltz they had themselves originated.

At the Winter Garden they revived the cakewalk, but under their skillful handling this was turned into a glorified thing which the originators would never have recognized.

Valentino as I Knew Him

Bonnie then opened her Montmarte, in the basement of the old Boulevard Café, and Rudy's salary was raised to the munificent sum of one hundred dollars per week.

As this was the year 1914, Italy had entered the war, and Valentino wanted to volunteer as an aviator, to learn which profession he spent all his spare time at Mineola. But when he offered himself to his country, he was rejected temporarily because of defective vision. Later, in San Francisco, he applied to Major Manchester, Commander of the British Recruiting Station but was told that he could not possibly pass the examination, and would only be sent back at his own expense. He had intended going to Canada to try to make the Royal Flying Corps.

Valentino and Bonnie Glass played their engagement at the Palace Theater and made a tour of the larger eastern cities. Then Bonnie opened the Chez-Fisher on 55th Street, which was very exclusive yet popular with the best people. Here they danced until she married Ben Ali Haggin and retired.

Joan Sawyer then engaged Valentino to dance with her during a vaudeville tour. Afterwards they appeared at Woodmansten Inn.

Although, as the world knows, Valentino was such a success as a dancer that he could have made

by S. George Ullman

dancing his career and doubtless a fortune at it, nevertheless he disliked it with his whole soul when it was placed on a commercial basis, and longed to get away from it as a profession.

Deep down in his heart was always the thought that, since he had made his one success in Italy at an agricultural college, he should do something worth-while with the knowledge thus acquired at such cost.

Hearing that California offered great opportunities, the wonders of that golden country being dinned in his ears, he joined a musical comedy called *The Masked Model,* because this was going to the coast. His salary was seventy-five dollars per week and traveling expenses.

In San Francisco he played with Richard Carl in *Nobody Home.*

Shortly after this he met Norman Kerry, who was the business representative for his wealthy father, but who disliked the whole thing so much that he was thinking of going into pictures, and suggested this to Rudy.

Having nothing in particular which appealed to him more, Rudy was agreeable, and set his heart on getting to Los Angeles.

But how? As usual he was out of money. He himself said he never could save, and I, as his business manager, know that this was no lie.

Valentino as I Knew Him

The transportation problem to Los Angeles was answered by an invitation from the late Frank Carter, husband of Marilyn Miller, who suggested that Rudy go with *The Passing Show*, in which Al Jolson was starring.

"Join us," he said. "We are doing one night stands to Los Angeles and there is always an extra berth on our train."

Al Jolson, being consulted, was also very friendly and confirmed the invitation, thus giving Valentino his trip to Los Angeles free.

Rudy told me that on this trip Frank Carter would not let him spend a nickel of his little hoard of money, insisting that he would need every penny of it when he got to Hollywood. This generosity on the part of Frank Carter established him as a prince in the estimation of Valentino, for appreciation was certainly one of Rudy's most notable qualities.

He was enormously pleased that Norman Kerry met him at the station, and, in spite of Rudy's protests that he could not afford it, insisted that he put up at the Hotel Alexandria, then the best in town, and start out by making a good impression.

It is a fortunate thing that the poor boy knew nothing of what awaited him. Having achieved some note as a dancer, a little more as an actor, and having made some new and influential friends

Rudy and two of his favorite dogs, both of which died shortly after the death of their master

by S. George Ullman

in the profession, he doubtless felt that all he had to do was to utilize a few introductions and thus be started on his career.

But Hollywood is *terra incognita* to one and all. The profession of motion pictures is strewn with the failures of those great in the professional, theatrical, literary and dramatic world.

Literally scores of artists, great in their own field, have come to Hollywood intent upon cashing in on reputations already secure in the East, and even in Europe, and have crashed to failure because the requirements of motion pictures were such that they could not qualify.

To succeed one must think in pictures, and this many are unable to do. Furthermore, all the large producing companies have an already-filled staff of men and women whose past experience has made them valuable, so that it must indeed be an outstanding figure or presence which can get by the Cerberus who guards the entrance to these studios.

Plainly speaking, it is a case of supply and demand; and there is always an over supply on account of the fact that Hollywood is the Mecca of all artists who hope, through the magic of pictures, to obtain a wider field for their talents.

Valentino's first job in motion pictures was as an extra, for which he received the munificent sum of five dollars a day, when he worked, and this

Valentino as I Knew Him

was not continuously. Thus his stay at the Hotel Alexandria was dramatically short.

Valentino was always very grateful to Emmett Flynn, who was the first director to employ him. The picture was *Alimony*, starring Josephine Whittel, who was then the wife of Robert Warwick. It is a noteworthy fact that working in this same picture, also as an extra, was a young girl named Alice Taffe. Later you saw her on the screen as Alice Terry in *The Four Horsemen of the Apocalypse*. Thus these two untried young actors reached fame at a single bound, in and through the same vehicle.

The author of *Alimony* was Hayden Talbot, and one day Norman Kerry introduced Rudy to him. Valentino told me that Talbot had not noticed him among the extras, but immediately upon meeting him said:

"You are a great type for a story I have in mind. If I ever write it and it is produced, you will get the part."

Rudy thanked him, but it was so much like other Hollywood promises that he wisely thought no more about it.

Naturally, after having secured the attention of Emmett Flynn Rudy was very hopeful. He had earned his first real money in pictures. He felt so sure the way had opened that it was difficult.

by S. George Ullman

for him to understand his inability to get constant work.

In company with thousands of others he tramped from studio to studio, beseiging doorkeepers and casting directors, and meeting with an indifference which breaks the heart of all except the stout of soul. He did not realize that, being so unmistakably foreign in type, he did not even fit into the ordinary extra class, which comprised mostly American types. Thus Valentino started with an even greater handicap than most beginners.

His money being gone, Rudy was forced to appeal to the generosity of Norman Kerry, who very willingly staked him; and he took a small apartment at Grand Avenue and Fifth Street.

It is interesting to think what might have been the result had Valentino not possessed a friend at this crucial time who was able and willing to give him the necessary financial assistance to keep going. Some are not so fortunate, and fall by the wayside or return home in despair, so that it is in reality largely due to the big-heartedness of Norman Kerry that Valentino reached a fame far surpassing that of his benefactor; who never, however, had the smallness to feel or exhibit the slightest jealousy but openly rejoiced in his friend's success.

About this time Baron Long opened the Watts

Valentino as I Knew Him

Tavern, a roadhouse on the outskirts of Los Angeles. He offered Rudy thirty-five dollars a week to dance there. As this meant eating regularly, Valentino was glad to accept this offer, and, as the tavern was a rendezvous for film people, Rudy had the secret hope in some way to attract the attention of a director, and go back to pictures.

His dancing partner was Marjorie Tain, who afterwards was featured in Christie Comedies.

Nothing in pictures came of this engagement, but Rudy did meet some very fine people from Pasadena, who suggested that the Hotel Maryland, one of Pasadena's most exclusive hotels, might be able to utilize his services as a dancer.

He followed up this suggestion, and the Maryland engaged him for one exhibition on Thanksgiving Day, when he danced with Katherine Phelps. They were so well received in their dance that when the proprietor, Mr. Linnard, returned from the East, he offered Valentino a permanent engagement. But the terms were so small that Valentino could not afford to accept them.

By a curious turn of fate, the very day that Rudy turned down the Hotel Maryland offer he accidentally met Emmett Flynn on the street. Flynn seized Rudy by the arm and told him that

by S. George Ullman

the story Hayden Talbot had written with Valentino in mind was about to be produced.

Flynn urged Rudy to go at once to see Mr. Maxwell, the supervisor of productions.

Wildly elated, Rudy flew to the studio as on wings. He found the part to be that of a heavy, an Italian Count.

"Will you play the part for fifty dollars a week?" asked Mr. Maxwell.

Would he?

With his usual hopefulness, Valentino imagined that this was the big chance which would lead straight on to fame. But, just here, the jinx blotted out his star momentarily. There was a fight over the negative. The camera men had not been paid and they had obtained a lien on the film, thus tying up the picture.

Later it was released and advertised in this wise:

RUDOLPH VALENTINO

IN

THE MARRIED VIRGIN

Chapter 3

Having thus unconsciously starred in his first part, although there was no intention of conferring such honors upon him when the picture was made, he naturally looked for a continuation of his good luck. But there was another long period of inactivity; in spite of his most persistent efforts, he could get nothing.

This astonished Valentino, who was not then inured to the vicissitudes of a movie career. He did not know that he might star in half a dozen pictures, and then suddenly find his services unnecessary.

Once more Emmett Flynn came to his rescue. Flynn, possessing finer feelings than some, rather hesitated to offer Valentino the part of an extra after he had played a lead. But he finally ventured.

"Would you be willing to play the part of an Italian Bowery tough?" he asked.

"I will play anything!" cried Rudy, who was then only too happy to get the seven-fifty a day to which extras had then been increased.

Rudy afterwards told me, almost with tears in

Valentino as I Knew Him

his eyes, that Emmett Flynn kept him on the payroll during the entire production, although he did not work every day.

Valentino never forgot a kindness.

About this time, Valentino caught the attention of Henry Otto, a director for Fox, who surprised upon Rudy's face one of those inimitable expressions which were afterwards to make him famous. Otto tried to impress upon the Fox Company the value of his new find, but failed.

Just here Mae Murray, and her then husband, Bob Leonard, whom Valentino had known in New York, came prominently into his life.

One day, on passing through their set, Rudy called out a gay "Hello" to Bob Leonard. His gallant bearing caught the attention of the artistic Mae Murray and, a few hours later, Rudy received, by telephone, an offer of the rôle of leading man in *The Big Little Person*, to play opposite Miss Murray.

It seemed that they had been searching for the right type to play this part, and Rudy had happened to walk on at the crucial moment. This fitted in excellently with Valentino's belief in his star of destiny.

It is impossible to describe the transport of happiness into which this plunged the volatile young Italian. Rudy was almost beside himself with

Valentino as I Knew Him

joy, as Mae Murray was then at the height of her youthful fame, and to be selected to play opposite her was like receiving the right hand of fellowship from the gods.

Little did Miss Murray, being a modest person, imagine to what heights she had raised the handsome boy. But this was indeed the first chance that Rudolph Valentino had had in a real picture. That he was afterwards starred in that picture with the horrible name, *The Married Virgin*, was due to the fame he had achieved between the filming of the picture and its release.

But with Mae Murray he was an honest-to-goodness leading man, and that he put his best efforts into her picture goes without saying.

He retained her friendship to the very end, for when, after divorcing Bob Leonard, she married Prince Divani, she invited Valentino and Pola Negri to be her attendants at her wedding, which was a secret one.

Bob Leonard remained Valentino's friend, and when he could no longer get Rudy into pictures he was directing, he recommended the young fellow to Paul Powell, who was about to direct Carmel Meyers in *A Society Sensation*. Valentino landed the part in his first interview with the manager, at a salary of one hundred and twenty-five per

by S. George Ullman

week. Rudy told me that Paul Powell was the first to say:

"Stick to it, and you will some day make a name for yourself."

Rudy never forgot such words of encouragement.

This munificent salary so went to the head of the youthful leading man that he went out and bought a used Mercer car for seven hundred fifty dollars, for which he agreed to pay a hundred down and fifty a month. But it cost him about twice that much to keep it in repair, so that, when it was finally taken away from him, because he failed to keep up the payments, he was rather glad to let it go.

Paul Powell liked Valentino so much in *A Society Sensation* that he engaged him for his next production, *All Night*, and was also instrumental in getting Rudy a raise to a hundred and fifty per week.

It was about this time that an epidemic of Spanish influenza broke out, closing all the studios and taking the last chance from Valentino to get work. He resisted the disease for some time, but finally came down with it and, although he had it in a severe form, he refused to have doctors or to take medicine, because he declared that he believed in neither.

Valentino as I Knew Him

Bryan Foy, one of the thirteen Foys, children of the famous Eddie Foy, about this time became Rudy's roommate, and he has told me that even at this time Valentino possessed the aristocratic bearing and grandiloquent manners which later were a part of his fame. Bryan also said that Rudy would starve in order to buy suitable clothes for his parts, being even at that time always meticulously dressed.

Earle Williams, then being at the height of his fame, offered Valentino a part in *The Rogue's Romance,* in which Rudy had to do an Apache dance. James Young was directing, and, since he had the sense to see that Valentino knew what he was about, he allowed the boy to stage the dance just as he pleased, with the result that it was a great success.

So much so, in fact, that Valentino got the idea of some day starring in the part of an Apache. This remained with him to such an extent that when he signed his last contract, under which he had a voice in the selection of his plays, he asked to have an Apache story written for him, which was done. Since this story was written entirely around Valentino's personality, the idea was very pleasing to him. It had been returned to the authors for some minor changes when he went East on our last trip. When Valentino was taken

by S. George Ullman

to the hospital and his recovery was expected by all, the authors planned to send the story east by the hand of Pola Negri, who was to have read it aloud to him during his expected convalescence.

Death put an end to these plans, as to many others.

James Young took a great fancy to Valentino. Having been a well-known actor of Shakespeare, and being a man of vision as well as of artistic ability, he saw the possibilities in this as yet unknown actor. It is my opinion that had not James Young had such tragic experiences in his life, he would now be one of the greatest directors in the motion picture industry. But his sensitiveness led him to take things too much to heart.

Valentino sensed this appreciation and idolized his director. Mr. Young once said to him:

"Rudy, you ought to be a great actor some day, for you have more ability than most."

These words put fresh courage into the young man's heart and Rudy told me later that many times, when he was discouraged and was wondering if fame would always remain just beyond his grasp, these words kept coming back to him, and he would say to himself, "I must have the stuff, I must! For Mr. Young is a great artist and knows ability when he sees it."

Thomas Ince was Valentino's next employer.

Valentino as I Knew Him

Although his salary was but seventy-five dollars a week, the money was so welcome at the time that it seemed a fortune.

Rudy's next call was from D. W. Griffith, and he owed this to another letter from Paul Powell. Griffith was starring Dorothy Gish in *Out of Luck,* and Valentino was engaged for the heavy.

Again when Mr. Griffith presented *The Greatest Thing In Life* at the Auditorium in Los Angeles, Valentino was engaged to dance with Carol Dempster in the prologue. This, at a hundred dollars a week, occupied Valentino for about three months, and earned him so much recognition from the public that, when *Scarlet Days* was shown at the Grauman Theater, he was also a dancer in that prologue.

It was through Douglas Gerrard that he began to have a part in the social life in Hollywood. Gerrard was a director, and entertained much at the Los Angeles Athletic Club. It was at one of these parties that Valentino met Pauline Frederick, and it was at a party at Pauline Frederick's that Valentino met Jean Acker, his first wife.

It was a case of love at first sight, and they were married almost immediately. Valentino was then working in *Once to Every Woman,* starring Dorothy Phillips.

His marriage to Jean Acker lasted but a short

by S. George Ullman

time, yet, in spite of the fact that they were divorced, they remained friends, each always saying kindly and appreciative things about the other. Indeed, I may say that the grief of Jean Acker, when it was known that Valentino was doomed, was one of the most genuine things I ever witnessed. Feeling that the end was so near, and knowing that Rudy's last wishes would have been even more kindly than those which he always manifested, I allowed Jean Acker to come to his bedside. He was unconscious and knew no one.

She had been his companion on many occasions during this last visit to New York, and I realized that there was a growing friendliness between them such as is often remarked with those who are about to die. Thus Jean Acker was the last woman to see Rudolph Valentino in life.

Three other pictures came in rapid succession to Valentino. *Passion's Playground,* starring Katherine MacDonald, in which he played the part of a brother to Norman Kerry, then as a heavy in *The Great Moment,* starring Margaret Namara, and again a heavy in *The Fog,* with Eugene O'Brien.

Imagine the surprise of Valentino when, after he had played these small parts, he was called upon to play the part of *Julio* in *The Four Horsemen of the Apocalypse.*

In my opinion June Mathis should sit forever

Valentino as I Knew Him

in the seats of the mighty for having had the vision to see Rudolph Valentino, first as the young South American tango dancer, then as the young soldier in the battle of Armageddon. She visualized him in the part so clearly that she fought for his appointment and won over all her opponents. Too much credit cannot be given to June Mathis for thus drawing back the velvet curtain for Rudolph Valentino in his Great Adventure, his ceaseless quest for undying Romance.

To Rex Ingram, super-director, whose artistry has just won for him international recognition, in the presentation of the Cross of the Legion of Honor for his accuracy and poesy in depicting French history, should go unstinted praise in the handling of that difficult novel of Ibañez. The haunting figure of Rudolph Valentino as *Julio*, lonely even when among the wheatfields of his South American ranch, lonely even in the drawing rooms of Paris when he struggled with the great problems of where his loyalty and allegiance lay, loneliest of all when in the trenches and on the battle fields of France he was alone with his God, was the one outstanding memory which world audiences carried with them from the countless theaters in which this marvelous picture was displayed.

Fifty years from now those who saw this picture

by S. George Ullman

in their youth will tell of it to little children, and old men sitting in their clubs, watching the smoke spiral upwards from their cigars, will hark back to the haunting sweetness and forever loneliness of that wistful young figure, whose beauty they will never have been able to forget.

To say that Rudolph Valentino was made by *The Four Horsemen of the Apocalypse* is to state the case too mildly. Rather was Vicente Ibañez made in pictures by Rudolph Valentino. For then, and not till then, was created the vogue for his books, for pictures. And I venture to say that this novel of *The Four Horsemen* later sold by the hundred thousand because of the association of Rudolph Valentino with the character of *Julio*.

I myself had read the novel before the picture was produced. It made upon me no particular impression, any more than can be said of any thrilling novel of its type. Yet when I read it again, after I had seen the picture, I wept over the tragic story of *Julio*, because to my mind he was Rudolph Valentino.

When the picture was planned, the part of *Julio* was not intended to outshine the others. Neither was it planned to be an all star production, but merely a super-picture, with every part adequately taken. But when the first rushes of *Julio* were viewed in the projection room, both June Mathis

Valentino as I Knew Him

and Rex Ingram were swept off their feet, and, seeing the possibilities which might come from featuring *Julio*, they began at once to build up the part, literally moulding the character of *Julio* to fit the haunting individuality of Rudolph Valentino.

I think that never before in the history of motion pictures has such a thing been so conspicuously done; a great tribute to the budding genius of Valentino.

After this he played with Alice Lake in *Uncharted Seas*. Then *Armand* with Nazimova in *Camille*.

It is amusing now to realize that Rudy got only three hundred fifty dollars a week during all three of these pictures, and that when, after *The Four Horsemen* was released, he asked for a raise of fifty dollars, he was told that Metro did not feel that he was worth it, nor could they afford it.

A peculiar thing about Hollywood is that it does not at once realize the success of its pictures abroad. A preview here, a short run there, is all that Hollywood knows of its greatest successes, so that Valentino was long in discovering the tremendous hit he was making in the East.

Valentino's first work for Famous Players-Lasky Corporation not only marked an increase in salary to five hundred a week. It gave him great

ack Dempsey refereeing an early morning bout with Gene Delmont

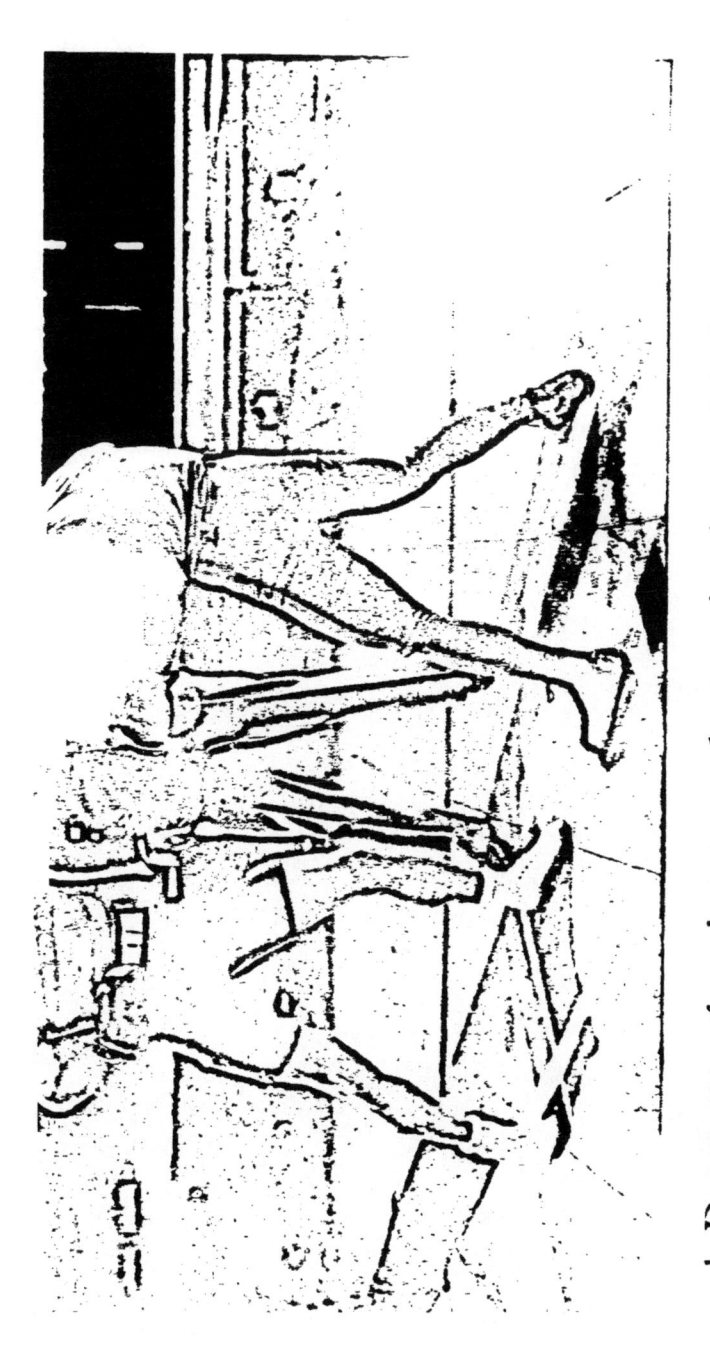

by S. George Ullman

satisfaction to work for that firm, which he regarded as among the finest in the motion picture industry.

The filming of *The Sheik*, with Agnes Ayres as his leading woman, gave happiness to all concerned, inasmuch as they believed that they were filming a masterpiece.

The sale of this book, by E. M. Hull, an English author, so totally unknown that it was months before the public discovered that its writer was a woman, had reached such proportions that not to have read *The Sheik* placed one in the moron class; and the enormous success of the picture is too well known to need comment.

At an increase to seven hundred a week, Valentino then made *Moran of the Lady Letty*, starring Dorothy Dalton, and, in order to obtain the offer of Famous Players-Lasky of one thousand dollars a week to play the lead in *Beyond the Rocks*, Valentino gave the company an option on his services.

Trouble began to brew with work on *Blood and Sand*. Rudy understood that he was to have Fitzmaurice for director, and that the picture was to be made in Spain. Whether his contract failed to call for this, or whether he was assured by some one not in authority to know that these conditions would be carried out, has never been satisfactorily

Valentino as I Knew Him

settled; but there is no doubt in my mind that Rudy was perfectly sincere in thinking that he had been badly treated when, with another director, the picture was made in Hollywood.

It is a strange commentary on the character of Valentino that, notwithstanding the artistic picture which Fred Niblo produced and its box office success, Rudy still clung to the idea that he had cause for grievance.

The fact remains, however, that beyond expressing himself with Italian volubility to all who would lend an ear to his alleged injustice, Valentino was too much of an artist to let his inner dissatisfaction interfere with his work. It is well known that he threw himself into the production of *Blood and Sand* with all the enthusiasm and energy of which he was capable. It was the comment of Charles Chaplin, after the death of Valentino, that he considered Valentino's acting in *Blood and Sand* as the greatest achievement of his career.

Blood and Sand was followed by *The Young Rajah*, which, although a vivid and colorful production gorgeously costumed and staged, was lacking in dramatic interest and was, on the whole, an inferior production. This Valentino resented, in the whole-souled manner of the true artist which Valentino undoubtedly was.

by S. George Ullman

Although he was getting a thousand dollars a week, the highest that he had yet received, the habit of some companies, of producing one or two great pictures to be followed by inferior films which Rudy called "cheaters," thus mulcting the public on the repuation of previous successes, was extremely reprehensible to him and filled him with fury. And the mounting trouble between Valentino and Famous Players-Lasky, he always declared, was because they did this, and made him the goat.

In the speeches which Valentino made while on his dancing tour with Natacha Rambova, which I shall explain further in detail a little later along in this narrative, he invariably made the statement that the quarrel with Famous Players-Lasky which resulted in their obtaining an injunction to prevent him from appearing on stage or screen for a long period, was a penalty he gladly paid in order to keep faith with his public. He openly accused Famous Players-Lasky of carrying out the nefarious practice of producing "cheaters" with every star they had under contract.

He also knew that if this practice had been kept up with him, his career would not be that continuously cumulative achievement which he so ardently hoped it would be. And he openly attributed the unnecessarily short-lived careers of

Valentino as I Knew Him

other stars in other companies to this dishonest and short-sighted policy.

How much of truth there was in these contentions of Valentino I myself am no judge. I set myself up as no arbiter. I am only trying to outline, in the simplest way possible, the real Valentino as he appeared to me during the all too short years in which I was privileged to know him.

But this I can truly state without fear of contradiction. Rudolph Valentino paid dearly and willingly for his determination to do what he could to elevate stars in the motion picture industry to what he considered was their proper and rightful status. He always declared that no one knew so well as the star himself or herself in what sort of a story he or she could best shine.

Furthermore, he contended most of all for the rights of stars to keep faith with their publics, and not to be exploited for the benefit of the producers regardless of the artistic careers of their stars.

In my opinion a grave injustice was done Valentino by his own attorney, who, in filing his answer in the law suit brought by Famous Players against Valentino for alleged breach of contract, laid stress on the lack of proper dressing room accommodations, as if this constituted the main count of his grievance. This gave the Famous Players attorneys a marvelous opening, of which they

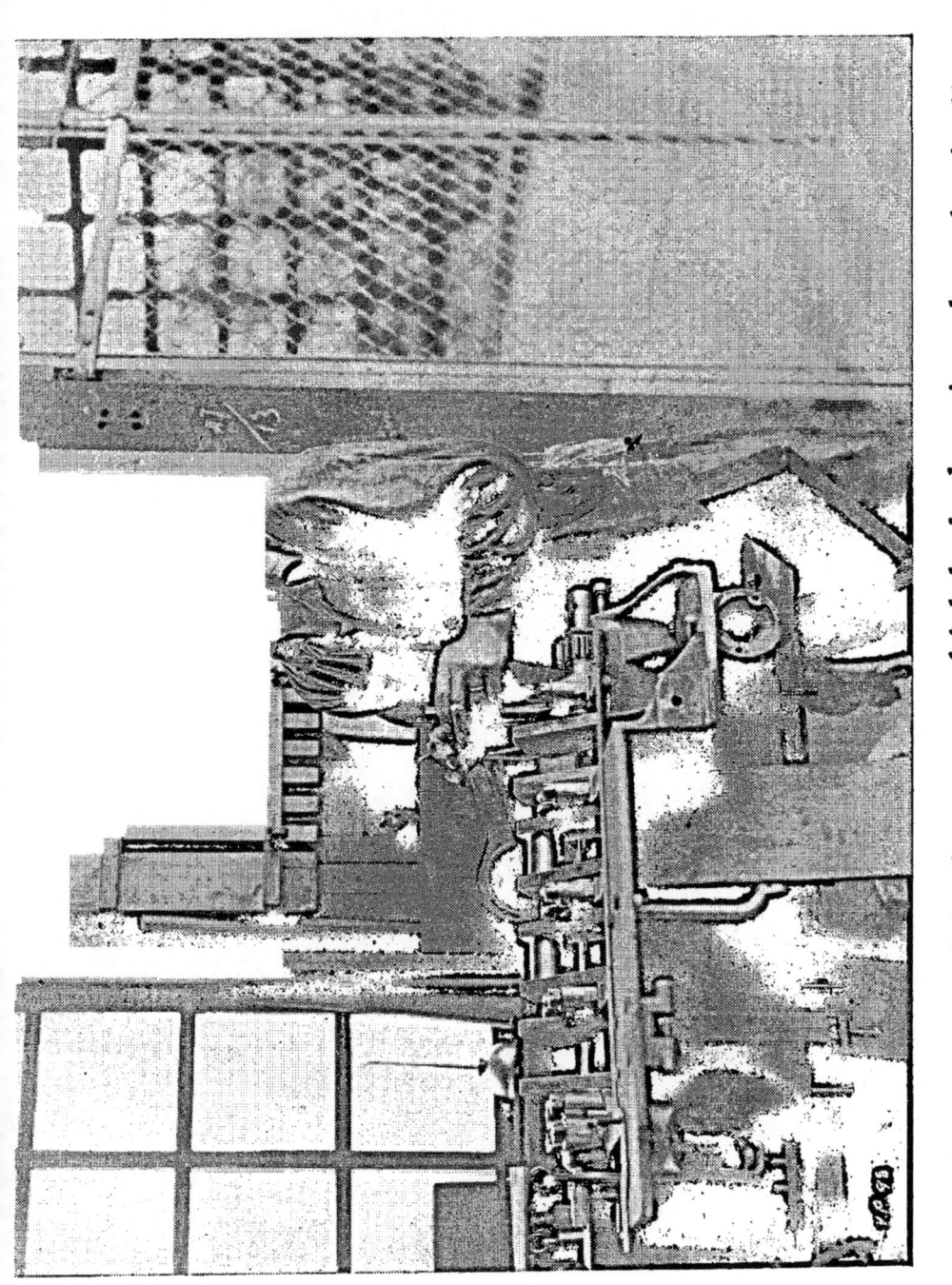

Valentino at work in the garage which he had equipped mechanically

by S. George Ullman

were swift to avail themselves. They played up what they were pleased to term Valentino's temperamental nature and hysterical demands, thus giving the public an entirely unfair and unjust picture of an earnest young actor whose sacrifices for his art entailed discomfort, ignominy, poverty and false representation in the press. Whereas I maintain that Rudolph Valentino was the only star in the entire motion picture industry who was willing to starve for an ideal.

His was an isolated example of the determination of all true artists to force justice and to maintain high ideals of dramatic art. These, when called *en masse*, constituted the actor's strike, famous in history, which resulted in the formation of that tremendous organization called Equity.

Chapter 4

It was previous to this troublous period, in fact, during the production of *Uncharted Seas*, that Rudy first met Natacha Rambova, whom he afterwards married.

She was then the art director for Alla Nazimova, and was designing gorgeous costumes for that eminent artist in Pierre Louÿs' *Aphrodite*. Rudy told me that he and Natacha did not speak the first time they saw each other, nor were they even introduced. Natacha, in her cool, detached way, calmly went about her business without so much as a glance in the direction of the proud young Valentino.

Possibly this piqued his vanity, for when Nazimova came over to the set where Valentino was working on *Uncharted Seas*, bringing Natacha with her, Rudy sought an introduction. But again he was met with an indifference to which he was not accustomed.

Every strong personality in man or woman will understand that this aloofness could not fail to intrigue so intense an individuality as that of Rudy. Possibly he himself did not realize this, but the fact remains that, from this time on, it

Valentino as I Knew Him

was observed that Valentino made persistent efforts to be with Natacha in what was perhaps an unconscious but nevertheless determined attempt to break down her reserve.

But at first Natacha was genuinely disinterested in Valentino. While younger in years, in experience she was much older than the lad. In the beginning her interest in him seemed to be motherly, or rather that of an elder sister.

When Valentino played *Armand*, with Nazimova as *Camille*, Natacha helped Rudy with his costumes, with the arrangement of his hair. In this simple fashion she gave the lonely youth a glimpse of what her sympathy might mean if ever she became his friend.

There is no doubt, however, that it was some time before Natacha finally viewed Rudy as a serious aspirant for her hand. And had it not appeared to her that her sympathy was needed, I very much doubt if she ever would have taken Valentino seriously, for he could not fail, on account of his youth and inexperience, to appear somewhat at a disadvantage.

As the acquaintance grew, these two young people discovered that they had much in common. Both were artistic, both possessed towering ambitions and both were very lonely, which last undoubtedly precipitated their romance.

Valentino as I Knew Him

Furthermore, both were interested in distinctive dancing. In this art Natacha possessed the skill which came from a long apprenticeship in interpretive and ballet dancing. But Valentino possessed a dramatic quality in his soul which caused every step in his dances to be forever memorable. Is it not true that his first step in his famous tango rivets the attention and brings, even to the most jaded, a certain retroactive thrill?

I believe that the way each reacted to the other's personality on the subject of dancing finally struck a spark in Natacha and caused her to think favorably of Rudy's suit. Once awakened, however, she began to see the beauties in his character, and this finally caused her to marry him.

Frankly, I say that never in my life have I seen two more beautiful creatures together than Natacha Rambova and Rudolph Valentino during the year in which they were engaged.

That Valentino finally completely won her affections was evidenced by the fact that, disregarding the year which should have elapsed before the decree of his divorce from Jean Acker became final, he married Natacha in Mexicali, Mexico.

About this time reëlections of politicians high in the legal department of Los Angeles loomed. And, as is always the case, hectic activity was manifest. Anxious for a political scoop, the Dis-

by S. George Ullman

trict Attorney's office pounced upon the marriage of Valentino as a marvelous example of the speedy justice it desired to depict.

Valentino was tricked into going to police headquarters on a Saturday afternoon; it was evidently the intention of the powers to clap him into jail and keep him there over Sunday. Doubtless other influences were at work. Those having it in for Valentino, for some cause or other, were at the bottom of this *coup de théâtre*. It amuses me to recall how ineffective these tactics proved; poor indeed must be the movie actor or actress who cannot call upon personal resources or the resources of their friends for bail in any amount.

In this case, it happened to be Douglas Gerrard who heard of Rudy's predicament and forthwith got in touch with his friend Dan O'Brien, Chief of Police of San Francisco, who was sojourning in Los Angeles.

O'Brien, at the telephone, said that, much as he sympathized, he did not have the necessary ten thousand dollars, the exorbitant bail imposed upon Valentino; but it so happened that Thomas Meighan was calling on O'Brien at the time and overheard this conversation.

Without knowing the identity of the friend whom O'Brien wished to serve, nor the name of the man at the other end of the wire, Tommy

Valentino as I Knew Him

Meighan, with the generosity for which he is famous, got O'Brien's attention, saying:

"Some friend of yours in trouble? How much do you need?"

Out of the corner of his mouth O'Brien replied:

"Ten thousand bucks! Got it?"

"No! But I can get it," said Meighan. "Wait here!"

With that he seized his hat and dashed out, returning in half an hour with a certified check for ten thousand dollars.

O'Brien took the check in his hand, looked at it and, with a quizzical smile, said:

"Do you know Rudolph Valentino?"

"Yes," said Meighan, "I do. Is he the fellow?"

"Yeah," said O'Brien. "What do you think of him?"

"I think he's all right!" said Meighan. "I like him. Regular fellah."

Still holding the check between his fingers, O'Brien said:

"Want to put this up on him, now that you know?"

"You bet!" said Meighan. "He'd do as much for me."

Which is the way that Rudolph Valentino was bailed out of prison on that Saturday afternoon

56

by S. George Ullman

and spent his Sunday at home, as was his custom.

At the first indication of this trouble, Rudy sent Natacha to her parents, at their place, *Fox Lair*, in the Adirondacks.

When he appeared for a hearing on this charge, he was able to prove that the marriage had never been consummated, and he was thus cleared of the charge of bigamy, but warned that he must not be remarried before Jean Acker's interlocutory decree became final.

Valentino then went East, where he and Natacha set up separate homes.

In the meantime, the suit of Famous Players-Lasky against Rudolph Valentino for alleged breach of contract was dragging its weary length along. The company finally secured a permanent injunction, forbidding Valentino to appear on stage or screen until the terms of his contract were fulfilled.

Chapter 5

I FIRST met Rudolph Valentino in the winter of 1922. I knew that he had had a disagreement with Famous Players, and that for some time he would either be at leisure or open to a good business proposition. I knew that he wished very much to marry Winifred Hudnut, or Natacha Rambova, as she now prefers to be called, and that for that reason he would need money. She was a very beautiful girl, with a marvelous complexion.

I, being essentially a business man, with an eye for advertising, conceived the idea of utilizing the spare time of this young actor, for to me he was not then the movie idol nor the great screen lover which in the last four years he has turned out to be. He was simply a good dancer, well known to the public, and with that magnetic personality which drew the feminine contingent. I knew also, as the whole world knew, that there was an injunction against his appearing on the stage or screen. But nothing was to prevent his appearing as a dancer, and this was my plan.

I was at that time connected with a beauty clay

But here Valentino has developed into the pop actor; in "The Conquering Power"

Valentino as I Knew Him

company and we needed spectacular advertising. I therefore suggested that we engage Valentino and his bride for a tour of the largest cities, to dance and to recommend our specialty as the reason for the lovely complexion of his bride.

This arrangement having been satisfactorily completed, Valentino and Miss Hudnut were married at Crown Point, Indiana, and came immediately to Chicago, where a special car, luxuriously fitted, awaited them.

I shall never forget my first meeting with Rudolph Valentino. Naturally, I was familiar with his pictures and thought of him as a handsome boy. I had no idea of his magnetism nor of the fine quality of his manhood. To say that I was enveloped by his personality with the first clasp of his sinewy hand and my first glance into his inscrutable eyes, is to state it mildly. I was literally engulfed, swept off my feet, which is unusual between two men. Had he been a beautiful woman and I a bachelor, it would not have been so surprising. I am not an emotional man. I have, in fact, often been referred to as coolheaded; but, in this instance, meeting a real he-man, I found myself moved by the most powerful personality I had ever encountered in man or woman.

This stirring emotion, which was as much a sur-

Valentino as I Knew Him

prise to me as it could have been to any one, was probably the reason for his enormous success upon the screen, for Rudolph Valentino was in the class of those few men and women who possess a tremendous individuality.

The appellation "personality" is too weak. That word may be applied with propriety to hundreds, even thousands, of men and women in every walk of life. But to sway multitudes by a mere gesture or a glance means much more.

Individuality is possessed by comparatively few. Great military leaders, who have commanded their armies to impossible feats of sacrifice and heroism, which the world has been unable to explain, have doubtless possessed a portion of this magnetic individuality. And therefore I, who greatly loved him, may be excused if I place Rudolph Valentino, after four years of intimate knowledge of his character, in the class of those truly great souls whose individuality was utilized in the cause of humanity, supplying romance to the gray drab lives of those to whom existence was nothing but a daily grind.

No one, privileged to read the pathetic, misspelled and ignorantly written letters which came to Valentino from his myriads of admirers, could fail to be impressed with the pathos of the admiration of these writers for the one who, to them,

by S. George Ullman

spelled Romance. It is said that Valentino's fan mail exceeded that of any other screen idol. But it is not fair to leave the impression that only the ignorant wrote to him. Among his letters were those bearing crests, monograms and insignia, giving evidence of the standing and intelligence of their writers, and breathing the most intense admiration of an actor who so passionately adored and represented Beauty.

In this, however, I have been referring to the last years of his life, whereas I must now go back to the first few days of my acquaintance with him and emphasize the fact that never for one moment did this man allow his name to be used in connection with the beauty clay. It was part of his contract that it should be exploited always as an adjunct to a woman's toilet, and this fact is only one of the strong indications I constantly had of the intense masculinity of Valentino.

He might wear a slave bracelet or rings, but he would wear them with the fine disregard of a European for what any one might think of his personal tastes. It is only American men who are sensitive to public opinion of their dress. No one who has traveled extensively can but be aware of the sublime confidence of the Britisher, the Continental and the Russian that their clothing is at all times suitable to the occasion and the weather.

Valentino as I Knew Him

They feel that it is nobody's business to criticize what they wear, and, if such criticism occurs, their surprise is genuine.

This Continental attitude Valentino shared, and he was constantly amazed that his apparel caused comment, even if favorable; for to him his adornment was but an expression of his moods. This, to him, was perfectly legitimate, and nobody's business but his own. Such an independent habit of mind, being a part of Valentino's confident individuality, was inexplicable to certain newspaper writers, whose comments indicated that they had never been beyond the confines of their home town.

Many of these impressions, which afterwards solidified into convictions, were formed during the conversations I had with my friend during the journey from Chicago to Omaha, which was to be the first stop of our tour. Here it was planned that Mr. and Mrs. Valentino appear for their first advertising performance. They were to dance, and afterwards Valentino was to make a little selling talk, attributing the beauty of his wife's complexion to the beauty clay.

Naturally, having conceived this tour, I counted largely on fair weather. But to my horror a fierce blizzard was raging over Nebraska, and I feared that few would dare its violence.

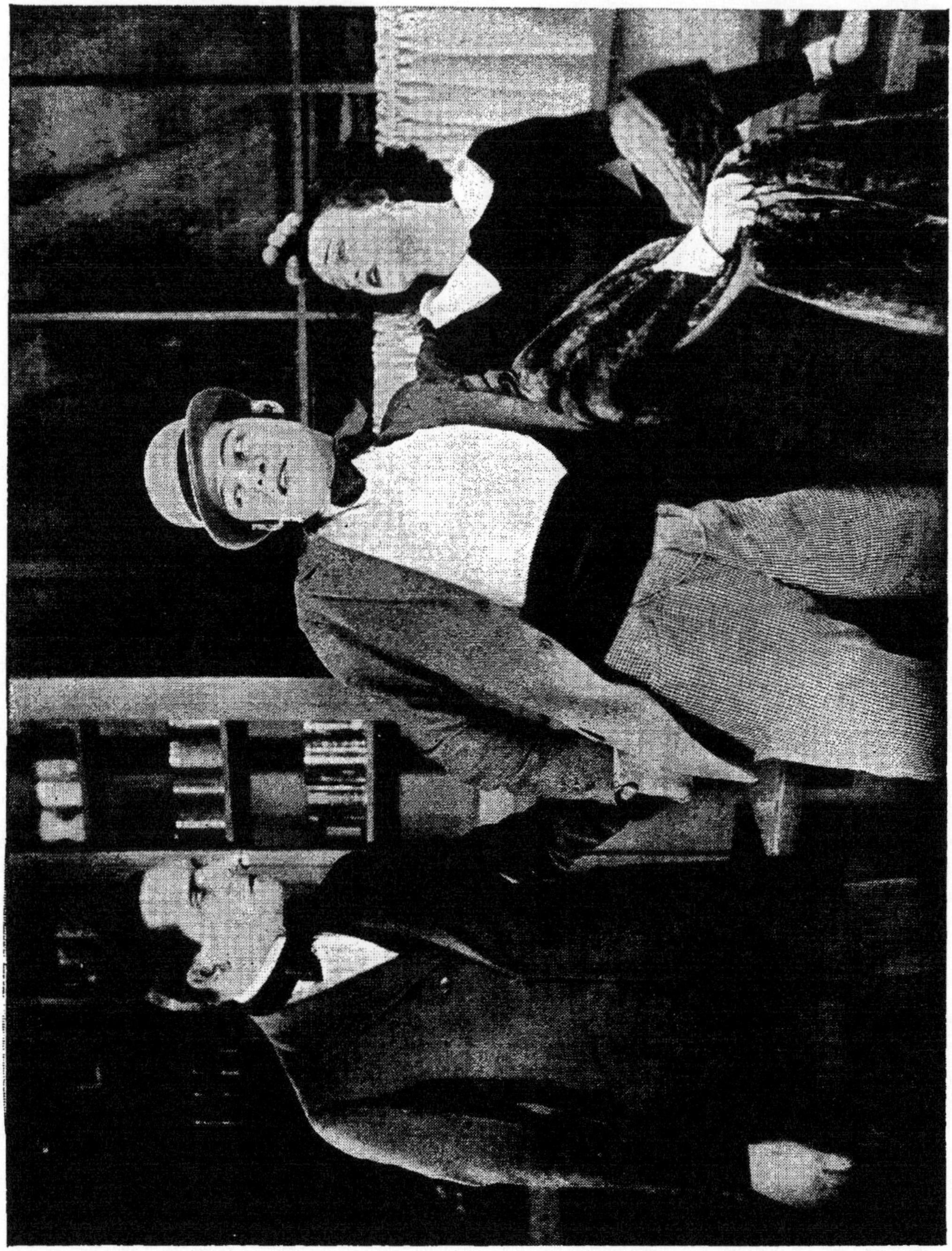

by S. George Ullman

Little did I know the effect of the advertisement that Rudolph Valentino and his bride would appear! To my surprise, the place was packed to the doors, and hundreds turned away. This was the first indication I had of the drawing power he possessed; but in the days to come I was to have it so impressed upon my mind that it ceased to amaze and became a thing to be taken for granted.

The success of our venture in Omaha was but a forerunner of that which attended these two dancers everywhere they appeared. Rambova, naturally graceful, had been taught by Theodore Kosloff, whose pupil she was for several years. So that, when Valentino undertook to complete her education in dancing, there was little left for her to learn. She was, and is, a rarely beautiful woman, possessing in many ways the inscrutable appearance of the Oriental as well as much of their fascination.

It was a wonderful thing to see these two exotic and graceful creatures dance. Their program consisted of the Argentine tango, which Valentino made famous in *The Four Horsemen of the Apocalypse;* they wore the original costumes. This was followed by another dance, a fiery, tempestuous thing which they originated themselves, and which partook of the qualities of Russia and the Far East. They always appeared to be dancing

Valentino as I Knew Him

for and with each other, for the sole joy of being in each other's company. They never seemed to realize that they had an audience, and this increased the thrill the onlookers obtained from watching them. And, if Valentino is credited with introducing a new style of love-making, much of it is due to the fact that he dared to be sincere in public and to allow all who would into the secret of the depth of his devotion.

Many actors spoil excellent love scenes by their self-consciousness. They are unable to forget their audiences; consequently they always appear to be acting. The lack of self-consciousness of the true artist caused Valentino to stand absolutely alone. He dared to express the utmost sincerity, the sublimest passion, without the slightest trace of self-consciousness; and for this reason he could not fail to be called "The Screen's Greatest Lover." But then again, he was supremely gifted in the fine art of being a lover, and this gift he frankly shared with his audiences.

This tour of the United States, in the interest of the beauty clay, consumed about seventeen weeks. It occupied the time which would have been spent on a honeymoon had not the necessity to earn money intervened. In November of the same year, this bride and groom sailed for Europe on a belated honeymoon, which possibly they were

by S. George Ullman

the better able to enjoy because of the strenuous time they had spent in earning it.

It was part of our contract that they select in each city a beauty who, for some reason, might be considered outstanding. We early discovered that, if Valentino made the selection, he would make more enemies than friends. So we decided to let the audiences themselves make the decision by their applause. In this way many a girl, by sweetness of disposition or personal magnetism or popularity, obtained the vote, whereas some, possibly more beautiful, but dumb, were obliged to take second place. In this selection we had no hand. In every instance the beauty was selected in accordance with the applause of her own townspeople. It is interesting to note that quite a few of these girls entered the movies or other professions because of publicity resulting from these contests.

I became aware of the tremendous drawing power of Valentino when I saw the crowds which assembled at the stations to greet him. Even at sidings where our train halted to let another train pass, crowds would gather. In Wichita, Kansas, I recall that the town took a holiday appearance. In other towns schools were closed so that the children might see Rudolph Valentino. To me it was a revelation, for I had previously had

Valentino as I Knew Him

no conception of his overpowering popularity. I was also surprised at his ability to make extemporaneous speeches. If he attempted a prepared speech he bungled horribly and made a general mess of it, but if allowed to talk as he would he was easy, natural, unaffected and dramatic. In Montreal, I remember that an enormous crowd had gathered to hear him and he made his first speech in English; then, realizing that this was a bilingual town, he repeated practically his entire speech in French, to wild, almost hysterical applause. I have seldom seen him create a more favorable impression or reach the hearts of the people more surely than he did that night through his linguistic ability.

I am also reminded just here of a question I once asked him. He was speaking to me of a Spanish novel which contained a story he thought might be adapted for the screen. I asked him what language he thought in, and he answered, "When reading a Spanish book, I naturally think in that language, but, since you have asked me, I find that I translate my Spanish thoughts to English when they concern the English making of pictures. In things concerning France or the French I would naturally think in French. Whereas, of course, concerning Italy and my life there I think in my

by S. George Ullman

native Italian. But always in America or England I think in English."

In Salt Lake City, which, by the way, was Natacha's home during her early childhood, one of the inevitable mistakes occurred which are bound to happen in any protracted tour such as ours. An enormous crowd had collected. The dance was to have begun at 8:30, but Valentino failed to appear. During two hours I kept the orchestra playing and made several appearances, assuring the audience that I knew Valentino was on his way; I must admit that I was roundly hissed. It was very hot, there were no seats, and the standing men and women were packed together like sardines. Their tempers grew momentarily more ugly, until they began to mill around in a manner to make me very uneasy. The cries and exclamations were of such a nature that I was afraid that when he did appear they might do him bodily harm. Suddenly, to my relief, at 10:30 he appeared. I warned him that the crowd was in an ugly mood and cautioned him to be careful. I shall never forget how he smiled at me, playfully pushed me aside, and walked out before that crowd, still in his street clothes. He explained to them that for two hours he had been trying to get through their traffic, and reminded them that they knew that this was impossible. This caused a laugh, and cries came from the crowd of, "Do your stuff, Rudy! You're all right!" With a smile and a bow he left them, and came into his little improvised dressing room, leaving the crowd pacified and receptive. Personally, I always thought he would make a good lion-tamer.

Chapter 6

FEW would believe, seeing the assured acting of Valentino on the screen, that he was inclined to be shy by nature, almost timid in approaching others. For example, I failed to become very closely acquainted with him until we had been together three or four weeks. I had observed that both Rudy and Natacha were interested in something supernatural. Just what it was I did not know. Afterwards it turned out to be automatic writing and a form of the psychic. Before making any move, they consulted this power. Not knowing this, I was at first surprised by the quietude with which they received what appeared to me to be startling developments. When surprising things occurred, I naturally expected them to share my own amazement. But this they seldom did. Instead, I would be very likely to hear something to the effect that they had expected it and knew it would come. For example, they had known that they were to go on a long trip, that they were to take a new business manager, and that Valentino would change his attorney. It turned

Valentino as I Knew Him

out that these things had come to them through automatic writing.

When Valentino became sufficiently acquainted with me to explain these things, he naturally wished me to share his interest in them. Being open to conviction, I very willingly listened and, to my surprise, I found that a number of things predicted by this psychic force actually came to pass.

It was in San Antonio, Texas, that Valentino, after many false starts, and some show of nervousness, first broached the subject to me of taking over his affairs and becoming his business manager. I refused. I had a family, whereas Valentino was $50,000 in debt and had an injunction against him which prevented him from appearing on stage or screen; his salary of $7,000 per week he owed many times over. Where, then, would my salary come from? He waved this aside and with a sublime confidence in his guiding star he told me that he would pull out of this, that he would make plenty of money, and that he wanted me to manage his affairs. But I could not see it that way. I needed to know where my income was coming from. Yet when, ten weeks later, I suddenly and without any further assurance decided to become Valentino's business manager, I looked for some expression of sur-

by S. George Ullman

prise at my *volte face*. Both Rambova and Valentino smiled inscrutably, and said it had been predicted before they embarked on the tour that they would change business managers and that I would be the man! These things at first rather gave me the creeps, but later, because of the sublime confidence of the Valentinos in their psychic control, I became less skeptical and more confident.

It must not be thought that Valentino was superstitious in any small and trivial way. He had no objection to spilling salt, walking under a ladder, whistling in dressing rooms, beginning a picture on Friday, or sitting down with thirteen at table. These things he ridiculed. The phychic never became a religion to him, but he yielded to its mesmerism more than to any other form. This was entirely due to the influence of his wife, who was a firm believer in the occult and initiated him into its mysteries. It was for this reason that she changed her name from Winifred Shaunessy-DeWolfe-Hudnut to Natacha Rambova. She believed that she would achieve fame under this new name.

When we reached New York, after more than seventeen weeks of continuous but luxurious travel, most of the time in grueling heat, Valentino insisted on my taking immediate charge. He had explained the entire situation to me. I had seen

Valentino as I Knew Him

the many leaks and weak spots in his efforts to clear himself of his business difficulties, which were nagging and tormenting him only because he did not in the least understand them. He was as puzzled as a child when things happened, and never knew what it was all about. For example, he was paying an attorney a $2,500 weekly retainer and his affairs were dragging along without any visible signs of improvement. But Valentino was perfectly satisfied until it was pointed out to him that the first thing he must do was to change lawyers and get one who would straighten out his affairs with Famous Players, thus enabling him to get back upon the screen. He was made to realize that no public dancing, however successful, was as dignified as appearance upon the screen. No sooner had this been pointed out to him than he insisted upon my going with him, directly to his house, and writing to the lawyer then and there. He was then living at 57 West 67th Street. I found that the ease with which he made this decision was again due to psychic control.

Just here occurred one of the most remarkable things which Valentino did during the four years of my friendship with him. He had been paid the last of his salary of $7,000 a week, and had deposited it in the Empire Trust Company.

by S. George Ullman

Since he was always lavish in his expenditures, it would have been most natural for this money to fade as quickly as dew before the sun. To my surprise, he told me that before leaving New York to make the tour he had been staked by a friend in the motion picture industry to a drawing account of $750 a week, until it had amounted to $11,500.

"I think I ought to pay this man in full because he was so kind. I want to pay this debt before I pay anything else," said Valentino.

I told him to use his own judgment. We went down to the Empire Trust, and he drew eleven one thousand dollar bills and one for five hundred dollars. Armed with this he telephoned the office of his friend. The secretary, evidently fearing a request for another loan, said that the man was in conference.

"I must see him! I have something to give him! And it is in cash!"

"Come right on up! You can see him!" shrieked the secretary.

That Valentino wished to repay his loan in cash indicated two of his strongest characteristics. One was that he enjoyed the feel of the crisp new bank-notes between his fingers. A check would not have meant nearly so much to him. Another was that he was like a child in his enjoyment of

73

Valentino as I Knew Him

the pleasure of surprising his friend with the entire amount, paid when least expected. Rudy was always a Prince. He loved the *Beau Geste.* While he was not in the least grandiose, nevertheless he got a great deal of pleasure out of parting with almost the whole of his savings, a thing inexplicable to a thrifty or selfish mind. This also indicates his belief in his guiding star, for, when I remonstrated with him, suggesting that he spread the amount over more of his indebtedness and later pay the balance, he said, "Oh, there will always be more."

And, truth to tell, more did come. For immediately the differences with Famous Players were amicably settled, he returned to their fold at a marked increase in salary. He made two pictures for them, one *Monsieur Beaucaire* and the other *The Sainted Devil,* thus completing his agreement with Famous Players.

In the meantime, before making these pictures, Mr. and Mrs. Valentino took their belated honeymoon trip and went to Europe in August 1923. If a motion picture could have been made of this idyllic journey, it would serve as a criterion for other brides and grooms to come.

Without a thought of business or financial complications, these two intensely beauty loving souls drifted leisurely from one capital to another,

by S. George Ullman

dividing their time mostly between Paris and Nice, where her mother and stepfather live in princely style at the Chateau Juan les Pins, overlooking the blue-waters of the Mediterranean. Rudy has often told me that some of the happiest hours of his life were spent in this chateau.

Though this is the playground of the aristocracy and close to the gaming center of the world, Monte Carlo, it is a curious fact that neither Mr. nor Mrs. Valentino was a gambler by nature, or found fascination in games of chance. Possibly this was because both, while not offensively so, were supreme egotists. This was less pronounced in Rudy than in Natacha. In fact, it was only by long association with Valentino that I came to discover that he thought the world was his oyster.

It is true that he frequently took chances so long as to make an ordinary gambler pale, but to his mind this was not gambling. It was simply acting in accordance with his supreme faith in the star of his destiny. He was no weakling. He never faltered. He never lost confidence in himself. It never occurred to him that possibly he would fail or become obscure. He knew without the shadow of a doubt that things would go well with him, and that the sun would always shine. And this reminds me to emphasize the fact that, like all Italians, he was preëminently fond

Valentino as I Knew Him

of the sun. He could not thrive, nor even live for long, in a country where gray days predominated. The day was made for him by the amount of sunshine it radiated.

He was never so happy as when playing like a boy, with his dogs on the beach. I have often been asked what Valentino did to keep his magnificent body in the pink of condition, and I have always replied, "I do not know that he ever did anything regularly." He had no daily routine religiously to follow. I always observed that his play was work. Instead of tossing sticks into the water for his dogs to fetch, Valentino used the dogs as sparring partners, pitting their strength against his in the possession of the stick, or racing with them along the sands.

When, however, he needed extra training for a picture, no one could be more assiduous than Valentino. Up at five o'clock in the morning, he would train with a professional for two hours before breakfast. It may amuse housewives to know that, even to serve so great a star, this habit was not relished by his servants, who growled after the manner of their kind at being compelled to change their habits. Here again the personality of Valentino was apparent. Growls and frowning faces disappeared as if by magic when he entered the room, and once again they were the will-

by S. George Ullman

ing servitors, devotion itself to his slightest wish.

I do not wish to indicate that the Valentinos were above visiting Monte Carlo for an occasional play. But it was always in the nature of an excursion to please friends. Many were the parties arranged when a dozen or score would go to famous resorts, where they amused themselves with the usual sport of others.

It is rather strange that Rudy did not gamble more, because his luck was proverbial. Again it seems to have been because he did not think it necessary. He did not crave excitement, therefore he found little pleasure in playing for high stakes. It was the wrong kind of exertion. He was dynamic at any form of exercise which disguised itself as play, for few could play harder than Rudy when he was so minded. Likewise, few could work harder. He possessed an almost uncanny and unbelievable control over his mind, body and nervous system. He could work in a studio for twelve hours. Then, if he had an hour and a half in which to rest, he could fling himself down, drop to sleep instantly, and awaken completely refreshed and ready for another siege of work.

I hope that I may be excused for comparing my friend with men to whom the world has granted a far higher place in historical achievement. Nevertheless, it will be recalled that great

Valentino as I Knew Him

military leaders, who drained their physical resources by long hours of strenuous and nerve-wracking work, were thus able to sleep. This to me is an indication of a form of greatness, of complete mastery over one's mind.

This naturally leads to mention of another characteristic. He absolutely refused to worry. If things went wrong or the future looked black, what did it matter? The sun would shine if you only gave it time! True, he often became excited; would flare up, into a momentary rage, would say unwise and indiscreet things. But in a moment all was forgotten. With a shrug he would roll the burden from his shoulders. To be sure, it always landed on mine, but what was that to Rudy? To his mind, that was what I was for. And again, he knew that the anxiety I could not help suffering was but temporary. His confidence in the idea that things would immediately turn favorable was supreme.

When they returned from their honeymoon, they were still radiant with happiness and, with characteristic energy, both threw themselves into the production of *Monsieur Beaucaire,* the first of the two pictures Rudy was to make for Famous Players. This was filmed at the Long Island studio and during its production the Valentinos lived at the Ritz-Carlton Hotel. I was with them

In front of the garage doors at Valentino's Hollywood home

by S. George Ullman

a great deal, and I could not help observing that Valentino so completely threw himself into the part he was playing that he was Beaucaire at home. To his wife his manners were those of the courtly Frenchman; even when talking business with me he was Beaucaire.

Also living at the Ritz-Carlton was Rudy's old friend, O. O. McIntyre, who is said to be paid more for each syndicated word than any other writer. Certainly he was, in Rudy's opinion, the most brilliant.

Valentino admired McIntyre extravagantly, and the two men were much in each other's company, despite the fact that McIntyre was Rudy's severest critic.

During the filming of *Monsieur Beaucaire*, McIntyre's criticisms were so constructive that many of them Rudy gratefully accepted and used.

The friendship of O. O. McIntyre and Rudolph Valentino lasted until death.

I am of two minds about a curious thing I observed in connection with his rôle of husband. Sometimes I think he was acting, but again, and to this view I incline more frequently, I think it was the inherent quality of Romance in his nature, which prevented him from ever letting down completely in the presence of his wife his self-imposed rôle of knight. By this I mean that he was always the gallant to his lady. I do not think that his wife ever saw him in a disheveled condition. Nor did I. Always perfectly groomed, dressed for the occasion, down to the smallest detail, whether in dinner clothes or negligée; there was always a fine quality of delicate reserve in him which could not fail to appeal to the fastidious in both men and women. Naturally this would appeal mostly to women possessing the common, or garden, variety of husbands, whose love for grubbing in the garden in disreputable clothes, and hatred of parting with comfortable shoes, often cause clouds to rise on the matrimonial horizon. Valentino never had any old clothes. Everything was new and the last word in fashionable attire. Even his lounging suit of black satin, with red lapels and stripes down the trousers, took an air of distinction from its wearer.

It was during the making of *Monsieur Beaucaire* that Natacha obtained her first real insight into the making of motion pictures. Before this she had been an art director for Nazimova, where her artistic ability was much in evidence; but she was never permitted any hand in the actual production. In the making of *Monsieur Beaucaire* she utilized her prerogatives, as the wife of the star, to the utmost, entering into the smallest details and assisting in an advisory capacity, sometimes to the embarrassment of the director. Rudy, still in the rôle of bridegroom, and having an over-mastering faith in his bride's ability to do everything perfectly, threw all his influence on her side. If Natacha sometimes presumed too far, all she had to do was to refer the matter in controversy to her husband, who immediately upheld her with a loyalty and a zeal not always wisdom.

Few women, however, will cavil at this knightly attitude of Mr. Valentino, the consensus of opinion among wives, I have observed, being that too often husbands slip rapidly, and without visible gradation, from the rôle of bridegroom into husband, becoming either too masterful or too run down at heel.

To the very end, when the unhappy divorce of these two wrecked the greatest and most lasting romance which, in my opinion, ever came to Valentino, he maintained his attitude of respectful subservience to his wife's opinions and pronunciamentos. If she said a thing, it became true as by the divine right of kings. That she accepted this as no more than her due was part of her complex as a supreme egotist. To her, the world was her oyster; in her opinion, there should always, also, be a man standing near, with a sharp knife, to open it for her. That she never evinced either appreciation or gratitude to Valentino when he

Valentino as I Knew Him

occupied this rôle was, again in my opinion, part of her nature, which she could not, and made no effort to, change.

That I thus analyze the character of Natacha Rambova is in no way intended to cast any aspersions on her ability as an artist, which she possesses in a marked degree. I am simply trying to explain to his myriad of admirers why Valentino's romance went on the rocks, to his great disappointment and lasting grief.

It is only fair to say that in my opinion the supreme love of his life was for Natacha. I base this largely upon what he said to me about her after she left California. Also upon the fact that, when in his last illness, he had me telephone from the hospital to her half-sister to ask when Natacha was expected to return from Europe. Had these two met, it is my firm conviction that they would have been remarried, provided Natacha had consented. Certainly, I believe, Rudy would have asked her, for the greatest happiness in Valentino's tragic existence was during his life with Natacha Rambova. This I know from his own lips. Remember, too, that the title of this book is Valentino As *I* Knew Him.

In the making of *The Sainted Devil*, the second and last picture under the Famous Players contract, a clash occurred between two very beautiful,

by S. George Ullman

talented and temperamental women, Natacha Rambova and Jetta Goudal, and it is to correct a false impression caused by idle gossip that I go into this matter at all. It was reported at the time that the clash was caused by Valentino's interest in Miss Goudal, and Natacha's jealousy therefor. But such was not the case.

Jetta Goudal was slated for an important part which required elaborate costuming. The French woman's exotic taste along this line is too well known to need comment. Without hesitation I declare that her imagination is nothing short of remarkable, and for this reason there was bound to be dissension in the ranks. While selecting her costumes, she soared to such heights that two eminent costumers practically washed their hands of her. In all likelihood it was because they were unable to carry out her desires.

On the other hand, the delays thus caused were assuming alarming proportions, so much so, in fact, that since Miss Goudal remained obdurate, the company was forced to substitute an actress who was more amenable to discipline.

Later, when Miss Goudal found herself replaced by another, she publicly expressed great bitterness and wrongfully attributed the cause to Mrs. Valentino, indicating that Rudy's interest in her

Valentino as I Knew Him

had caused Mrs. Valentino such jealousy that the French woman was forced out.

If Jetta Goudal really believed this to be the truth of the matter, I can only say that she was very much mistaken. For at this time, and indeed all during his marriage to Natacha Rambova, Valentino had thought for no one but her. His love for her was so great that he never resented her dominance, nor even her interference in his business career. In his mind her taste and judgment were perfect and beyond question. It is also to be remembered that at this time the Valentinos had only been married about a year.

Chapter 7

With the release of *Monsieur Beaucaire* and *The Sainted Devil* a most extraordinary fact was forced upon the consciousness of the world, to the effect that upon the absence of Valentino for two years, his return to the screen was heralded by unprecedented popularity. Crowds flocked to see him in these two pictures, and both were enormous box office successes.

It is unique in the history of motion pictures. Never an actor nor actress, having left the screen for such a length of time, returned to such overwhelming ovations. This proved that the hold of Valentino upon his public was never lost, and the truth of the adage, "Absence makes the heart grow fonder," was marvelously evident in his case. For he returned to a more admiring and much larger audience than he had ever enjoyed before!

This phenomenon should set at rest forever the tongues of those who claim that Rudolph Valentino was merely a handsome Latin type who enjoyed a vogue, or who had become a temporary fad.

The fact of the matter is that his public loved

Valentino as I Knew Him

him and remembered him through sheer inability to forget so engaging a personality. Yet, further than that, he was a very great artist and wonderful actor, for a vogue, no matter how violent, is but temporary at best.

The American public, in spite of certain disparaging statements to the contrary, is fairly discriminating; and, in the long run, its final judgments may safely be depended upon. It may be misled; temporarily it may follow a blind lead; but finally it returns to its true gods. Therefore, any man who establishes a permanent hold upon its affections, such as box office returns and fan mail proved Valentino to have had, presents this truth in a manner never to be gainsaid.

If the proof of the pudding is in the eating, Rudolph Valentino was in a class by himself. No actor, past or present, was ever so beloved. I make these statements from a first hand knowledge of the scenes and episodes which took place, not during his life so much as from the moment the news of his sudden illness was flashed over the wires by telegraph and cable to the four corners of the earth. From the four corners of the earth messages came winging, to show that those who loved him were the humblest shop girl and the errand boy and also they who sit upon the seats of the mighty.

by S. George Ullman

So great was this love that, although at the time a certain resentment was felt in his native land, when he was forced to renounce his allegiance to his beloved Italy in order to become an American citizen and loyal to the land in which he had found his early and great success, all differences of opinion were erased by death. From the great Mussolini came a giant wreath which was laid upon his casket by reverent and loving hands; while Fascisti and Anti-Fascisti quarreled for the right to maintain an honor guard above the remains of their beloved fellow-countryman.

Tributes such as came to Valentino during his life and after his death could have come from no one reason. They came from the combination which I wish to stress: his ability as artist and actor, his vivid, engaging and heart-gripping personality.

It was always inexplicable to me why Natacha Rambova seemed to feel the indefinable charm of her husband's personality so little. Other women, who were his friends or more, would have yielded to its spell with the generosity of more ardent natures. But Natacha was conspicuously self-centered, and therefore in my opinion she was congenitally unable to feel much enthusiasm for the individuality of any one except herself. This must not be considered as an aspersion upon her

Valentino as I Knew Him

mentality. She was born with this complex, in my opinion, and never seemed, even in her married life, to make any effort to change.

At first, she did indeed appear to be fond of her husband, and to yield somewhat to the glamour of his individuality. But as soon as, through his courtesy, she began to be initiated into the mysteries and complexities of the actual manufacture of an important motion picture, and she began to have a dawning understanding of its methods, this slight knowledge so fed her ambition to be author, artist, producer and sole critic, that her obsession mounted to her brain like the fumes of strong wine. She began then to write day and night a picture in which her husband was intended to star. But that which seemed to be wifely devotion was in reality but the step necessary to be taken to place her in the supreme position she so ardently desired. And, I feel, from that moment dated

'That little rift within the lute,
Which by and by shall make the music mute,
And, ever widening, slowly silence all.

From the moment of Mrs. Valentino's entrance into the motion picture industry, she began, it is my opinion, to lose her interest as wife to Valentino and to become more and more occupied with her

by S. George Ullman

passion to be a power in the motion picture world. For, when the time came to choose, she chose the solitary path to selfish grandeur, and broke the heart of her husband.

For this I have never blamed her. I felt that she had yielded to her selfish desires. Never having learned the meaning of self-control or self-sacrifice, she could not do otherwise.

Mrs. Valentino became the business manager of her husband as soon as she married him, and her extravagance has wrongfully been considered a contributory cause of the divorce. But this is unfair to her. Rudy was not quite as extravagant as she. His sublime confidence in the star of his destiny caused him to spend money like water, and to incur debts which would have appalled a more conservative man. Had his wife spent ten times the amount she did, he would have applauded her judgment and mortgaged his future to gratify her whims.

It must be remembered that up to the time of the tour advertising the beauty clay, and the completion of his contract with Famous Players, which was followed by a contract with the Ritz Carlton Pictures, Valentino had never earned money in such generous sums. Therefore, his indebtedness of approximately $100,000 in attorney fees and other miscellaneous debts should have withheld him from unbridled extravagance. That it failed to do so did not so much spell failure to realize his financial responsibilities as it stressed his indestructible faith in himself as the captain of his soul and the arbiter of his destiny.

Had he lived, I would share his optimism, for I firmly believe that another ten years of a success which his past achievements would justify us in expecting, would have made him the richest as well as the most successful artist of the screen. I am constrained to believe this from the rapidly increasing value of his estate.

During their dancing tour the Valentinos signed an option on a proposed contract offered them by J. D. Williams. This option Mr. Williams, unknown to Valentino, took to Famous Players and hypothecated the proposed services of Valentino for the financing of those pictures for the production of which a new company was to be formed.

This company was later organized and known as The Ritz Carlton Pictures, Inc. The contract gave the Valentinos that power to select their own stories, which was one of Valentino's quarrels with Famous Players.

This power gained, it was Natacha's intention to select for the first story *The Scarlet Power*, subsequently called *The Hooded Falcon*, which was her own work. She used for this the pen name

by S. George Ullman

of Justice Layne. It was a story of the Moors in the early history of Spain. It was estimated that the production would cost between $850,000 and $1,000,000, and at this time all concerned seemed to have been unaware that it was the intention of the financial backers to limit each production to a maximum of $500,000.

Armed with permission to browse at will among the art treasures of Europe and to purchase props for the new picture to the extent of $40,000, the Valentinos gayly took ship and sailed for Europe in August 1924. Their wanderings took them through Spain, where Mrs. Valentino purchased approximately $10,000 worth of Spanish shawls and $10,000 worth of ivories, as well as double this amount in miscellaneous expenditures for their trip. Another $40,000 was spent in props for the new picture, consisting mainly of original Moorish costumes and jewelry.

Upon their return the Valentinos took a long term lease upon an apartment at 270 Park Avenue, at an enormous rental. Hardly had this transaction been completed and the apartment lavishly furnished, when the hitch in these plans took the startling form of lack of studio space to produce such an elaborate picture in New York. This forced the Valentinos to give up their plan of living in New York.

Valentino as I Knew Him

They retained the apartment, however, for commuting purposes between New York and California, and came to Hollywood, where they occupied the palatial home of Valentino on Whitley Heights.

Soon after their arrival it appeared that the plans for producing *The Hooded Falcon* must be temporarily abandoned, and Mrs. Valentino was given to understand that, for the production of so elaborate a picture as hers, more time must be spent in preparation.

Another story had been selected by Williams, although, by the terms of the contract, this was the prerogative of the Valentinos. This story was *Cobra*, taken from the successful stage play of the same name.

Valentino, with his unerring sense of discrimination, realized immediately that his part in such a picture was not suited to his best efforts, nor to his lasting fame.

Nevertheless, after having registered his disapproval and found it ignored, rather than cause any unpleasantness so early in his association with the company newly formed for him, he yielded, and a picture was made which amply bore out his reaction. While a picture with Valentino in the principal rôle could not at this time fail to be a

by S. George Ullman

box office success, it did not come up to the mark previous Valentino pictures had set.

Those were the days when the Valentinos were the happiest. Not only was their home life idyllic, but Natacha had practically full control at the studio during the making of *Cobra*.

I was production manager and, yielding to what I knew were Rudy's chivalric wishes in the matter, I allowed the reins of control to slip more and more from my own grasp, and to pass into hers, which I must admit reached greedily for them.

To her credit be it said, however, that she exercised to the fullest, in the making of this picture, her remarkable ability as an artist. To be sure, certain explosions occurred, one of which resulted in the changing of camera men right in the middle of the picture, which, even to the lay mind, would appear hazardous, but which did not harm the picture in this instance. This she could not forecast; it simply goes to prove that once in a while the expected does not happen.

To achieve her artistic success, Mrs. Valentino obtained the services of some of the greatest geniuses in the profession; one and all, I saw these men pass under the spell of her personality and yield up to her the greatest treasures of their art. This brings me to the subject of this woman's amazing fascination. Not only was her taste in

Valentino as I Knew Him

dress an eye-arresting thing, Oriental, exotic, sometimes bizarre, but her costumes invariably added to the almost sinister fascination she was able to exert whenever she chose.

Those whom she disliked and ignored, very often hated her. But upon any one on whom she bent her attention for any length of time, or whose allegiance she desired to secure, to serve her own ambition, or to forward any project of her own, she exercised to the fullest her uncanny ability to charm. Men seemed wholly unable to resist her, but yielded to her spell without a struggle. Of women friends she had few. Possibly Nita Naldi and Nazimova were conspicuous exceptions. As an example of the length to which even women would go for Natacha, Nita Naldi, even when a picture contract called for her services in New York, remained in Hollywood to accommodate Natacha Rambova, to play a part in Natacha's famous venture *What Price Beauty*, to which I will return later.

Rudy, although he must have been aware of this pronounced habit his wife had of fascinating her victims, never showed the slightest jealousy, nor seemed really to observe it. This was partly due to the fact that, while Valentino gave no evidences of conceit, his confidence in his ability to fill the

When Valentino returned from Europe in November, 1924, he had to shave off the famous beard

by S. George Ullman

picture was such that he never imagined it was necessary to become jealous.

This also is a quality of great egotists which Valentino's charm prevented from ever becoming conspicuous or even noticeable.

Just as in *Monsieur Beaucaire* Valentino took up fencing, so in *Cobra* he took up boxing.

During this time he was in the pink of condition, and seldom arrived on the set later than six o'clock in the morning. He would then box for two hours with his sparring partner, Gene Delmont, who at that time was appearing frequently at the American Legion Stadium in Hollywood.

Rudy's high powered Voisin, a French car, was always in waiting. He would jump in and drive himself home for breakfast, reappearing at the set in less than an hour, eager for work. To these luxurious habits of Valentino is due one thing for which all stars should be eternally grateful, and this is the building of bungalows on the studio lot for their exclusive use. Rudolph Valentino's was the first of these to be constructed, and he was the first to insist that the treatment of a star should be any different from the rest of the cast.

I have so frequently been asked concerning my friend's fine physical condition and tremendous strength, that I am reminded to say that he developed this himself. When he arrived in

Valentino as I Knew Him

America, he was only a well-formed boy, with possibly a little more than the ordinary strength. But with this he was not satisfied. It was one of his traits never to be satisfied with mediocrity. In whatever line of effort he was constrained to appear, it was always his ambition to excel. And such was his popularity that even the greatest boxers and gymnasts would freely give him encouragement and instruction.

Jack Dempsey was one of his greatest admirers, and not infrequently the two put on the gloves together.

It was to be expected that Valentino would wish to excel in horsemanship, since his father was a member of one of the crack regiments of Italian cavalry, than which there are no better riders in the world.

Valentino had magnificent horses. Some were gifts, some he himself imported. He was particularly picturesque upon Ramadan, a white Arabian stallion. Though perhaps he looked equally well upon a fiery black charger named Firefly.

Rudy was an enthusiasitc member of the Breakfast Club, that unique organization which entertains distinguished visitors to Hollywood, and which staged a memorial service for Valentino which I will describe later on. The Breakfast Club is largely equestrian, and there was never a

by S. George Ullman

more gallant figure than that of Rudolph Valentino, in his immaculate riding clothes, galloping over the hills in the early California sunshine.

He was particularly fond of stunts. He rode a great deal with his friend, Mario Carillo, who was formerly an Italian cavalry officer, and these two would put Rudy's horses through all manner of evolutions, jumping hurdles, rearing, water jumping and descending and ascending steep grades.

A man who is fond of children and animals is generally tender-hearted. Valentino's penchant for dogs, horses and babies is almost too well known to require comment. He was more popular with my children than I was myself. They would greet him with screams of joy, rush to his arms, the little one crying out, "Swing me up, too, Uncle Rudy!"

On the journey from which he never returned alive, our first stop was in San Francisco, where Mayor Rolph presented him with a beautiful water spaniel, with long silky black hair. Nothing could have pleased Valentino more, and he immediately insisted upon being photographed with the dog. Rudy was very anxious to take this latest acquisition with him to New York, but, fearing that the confinement of a long journey and the intense heat then raging in the East would cause

Valentino as I Knew Him

the dog suffering, he unselfishly sent the little fellow to his kennels in Hollywood, where the dog received the best of care, awaiting his new master's return. This dog I personally brought back to Mayor Rolph only recently, and this fine gentleman and his charming wife again brought back to me the wonderful hold Rudy had on the affections of the world, for, with tears in their eyes, these folks assured me that they could never part with this dog, and intended to keep it always in memory of their friend Rudy.

Chapter 8

Upon the completion of *Cobra*, the Valentinos went down to Palm Springs, for a little rest. Palm Springs is about one hundred and fifty miles from Los Angeles, just on the edge of the desert, the San Jacinto mountains rising steeply against the western sky. Although the hotel, The Desert Inn, was a most fascinating place in which to stay, with its bungalows clustered around the main hotel, and the beautiful lawns broken here and there by ramadas with their thatched roofs and open fireplaces, the Valentinos preferred to stay with their friend Dr. White, in whose attractive desert home they found sanctuary.

The sandy trails, sage brush and desert loneliness seemed to invite Valentino, and he spent much time riding, either alone or with his wife. When evening came, he always made a point of climbing the mountain in back of the hotel, to watch the changing colors of the sunset on the desert sands.

Gorgeous colors and rich materials always intrigued Valentino's beauty loving soul. Thus he would watch with enthusiasm the colors from the

Valentino as I Knew Him

setting sun as they stretched across the sands, turning from gold to crimson and interspersed with those blues and purples which are seen only on the desert.

In these moods the desert was Valentino, and Valentino was the desert. The same look would come into his eyes as I later saw upon the screen in *The Son of the Sheik*. When I saw him he was not acting. He did not even know that I watched, and it was thus that I knew. After once seeing him in what he supposed was a lonely vigil, I realized why it was that he was so great in the rôles of *The Sheik* and *The Son of the Sheik*. In my opinion he was more at home in these two pictures, and far greater in them, than in any others in which he appeared, always with the exception of his character of *Julio* in *The Four Horsemen of the Apocalypse*.

While these two lovers were enjoying themselves at Palm Springs, preparations were going on at the studio for the filming of *The Hooded Falcon*. Valentino, catching the enthusiasm of his wife, was looking forward with keenest anticipation to the performance of his rôle as a young Moor.

It will be remembered that when Valentino returned from Europe he was wearing a beard. Battles have been fought changing the destiny of a

by S. George Ullman

nation which created less excitement than the news that Valentino was wearing a beard. Newspapers everywhere commented upon the fact, and general disapproval was expressed, showing that his public desired to see him as the clean-shaven youth which he had so endeared to his picture public.

Likewise, it is my opinion that being obliged to darken his skin somewhat in order to play the rôle of a Moor would greatly have distressed many of his youthful admirers, so that, when rumbles of disharmony began to reverberate through the business offices, and whispers began to circulate that a disruption was near, I was perhaps less disturbed than some, feeling as I did that the fame of Rudolph Valentino would not have been materially increased by the production of *The Hooded Falcon*.

Finally came a letter from J. D. Williams, president of The Ritz Carlton Pictures, Inc., in which he said that he was not willing to go on with the production, fully realizing that in so doing he was breaking his contract with Valentino.

This ultimatum I conveyed to the Valentinos by telephone, whereupon Natacha declared that she would come immediately back to Hollywood, leaving her husband at Palm Springs. Naturally, I expected a storm. To my surprise, she appeared calm, indifferent to the breach, and even content

Valentino as I Knew Him

to have eliminated what I afterwards discovered to be what she considered the efforts of the Ritz Carlton to dictate to her and to relieve her of supreme command.

Thus, when I intimated that a new contract with Joseph M. Schenck was under consideration, she welcomed the suggestion, believing that in this new venture she could assume her rightful rôle of dictator general.

After I had had a conference with Natacha which lasted a day and a half, she returned to Palm Springs, leaving me to complete negotiations with Mr. Schenck. When the contracts were ready to sign, the Valentinos returned from Palm Springs, and Natacha then discovered that, in order to obtain this contract, Rudy was obliged to promise that she was to have no voice whatsoever in the making of any pictures which it called for.

Naturally, this was a tremendous blow to her ambition. Her plans and aspirations were to produce bigger and better pictures. Under this new contract she could not do as well as under the one which was abrogated.

It must be admitted that Mrs. Valentino possessed a great deal of common sense, for, in spite of the fact that *The Hooded Falcon* was her brainchild, she yielded with considerable grace to the inevitable, fully realizing what it meant to her

by S. George Ullman

illustrious husband thus to be taken into the fold of United Artists.

After the contract was signed, the Valentinos again returned to Palm Springs, while a search was instituted by the Schenck organization for a suitable vehicle for Rudy's next picture.

A story was finally discovered in a novel by Pushkin, the famous Russian novelist, from which the picture, *The Eagle,* was evolved. In the making of this picture Valentino exhibited a splendid coöperative spirit. Gorgeously costumed, he appeared first as a Cossack in the army of the Czarina, Catherine of Russia, then as an outlaw, and, for a disguise in order to meet the girl of his choice, he masqueraded as a French tutor.

Costumes were enormously becoming to Rudy. In ordinary golf clothes, or the habiliments of everyday mortals, he came as near to being commonplace in his looks as it was possible for one of his extraordinary beauty to be. Yet put him in puttees, riding breeches and a silk shirt open at the throat, and he was the Valentino of the screen.

To my mind he was less effective as a Frenchman than as a Spaniard, an Italian, a Cossack, or an Arab. The dainty ruffles, laces, and silks of a Beaucaire were less suited to him than the burnoose, the brilliant sashes and the sandals of the desert.

Valentino as I Knew Him

Valentino, at Palm Springs, began to be bombarded by his wife's argumentative questions as to why she should not be allowed to make a picture on her own. At first Rudy demurred, because his finances were not at that time in condition to stand so great a drain. But he naturally wished to advertise to the world his wife's ability. He had no more jealousy of her genius than a child. It never occurred to him that the best that she might do could in the least detract from the radiant sunlight of that public's approval in which he habitually basked.

Even though it may appear to cast aspersions on the sex to which I myself belong, I must admit that so many artists have been jealous of their wives' ability that I must stress Valentino's freedom from this form of self-love. To be sure, it came partly from his own absolute self-confidence and the belief that no one could possibly approach him in the perfection of his person and his art, but it likewise eliminated the friction which has wrecked so many other marital barks on the stormy oceans of I and my and thee and thine.

Nevertheless, at this time, I observed that Valentino's nerves were beginning to fray. Always unwilling to quarrel with his wife, unable to answer satisfactorily his wife's arguments, he took to spending whole days riding alone on the desert,

by S. George Ullman

galloping over its sands in a mad effort to escape the silky voiced persistence of a woman he still ardently loved.

Finally I received an imperative summons over the telephone to come down to Palm Springs immediately. So urgent was this request of Rudy that I drove the entire distance in a pitiless blinding rainstorm, to find what new trouble had arisen. I must have driven through the rain, for upon my arrival I found Rudy out on the desert somewhere upon his horse, and Natacha confined to the house with a sprained knee.

She was surrounded by books and magazines, drawings and plates, and she immediately took up with me the subject of her making an independent picture at a very small cost, her object in so doing being to show the motion picture world that she could make a commercial picture as well as an artistic success.

Of course I gave her every bit of advice I could concerning pictures, and concurred with her in the thought that inexpensive pictures were commercially practical, if she could make them.

With all the confidence in the world, she assured me that she could. I was still somewhat skeptical, and, when Rudy came in, I referred the matter to him. I at once saw that the nerves of both were drawn fine. In fact, I may say that they had begun to pull apart, and it was only by his yielding to her in this matter that an immediate catastrophe was averted.

By this time, Valentino had discovered that his wife's determination to achieve a thing was not to be lightly set aside. He knew, as well as I did, that it would be much better if his mind could be concentrated on his own work and not distracted by the anxieties and inevitable problems of an untried venture such as Natacha wished to undertake.

But her insistence, silky and soft voiced though it was, prevailed; a thing which those who know her realize was inevitable. I was distressed to see the signs of nervousness which Rudy displayed, knowing full well that this stay at Palm Springs was intended as a period of rest before the arduous job of portraying *The Eagle*.

Nevertheless we gave up like good little boys, and reached a compromise with the lady by giving her her own way.

I had previously had a long talk with Rudy, during which we discussed the matter pro and con, realizing its inadvisability. But Valentino assured me that, in the cause of peace and of rest for himself, he must give in and do as she wished. I could see that, combined with this desire for a cessation of hostilities, if these bloodless arguments could be called that, there was a very genuine de-

by S. George Ullman

sire, deep down in his heart, to make his wife happy. Likewise a determination to go any length to achieve this.

Before I left, it was decided to allow Natacha to try her hand at an independent picture, which she declared could be produced for approximately $30,000. That under her unbridled artistry the cost more nearly approached $100,000 caused more friction all around.

Upon our return to Hollywood, plans were at once set in motion for the production of Natacha's picture, *What Price Beauty*. This clever story Mrs. Valentino wrote herself. She was thoroughly familiar with her subject, being the step-daughter of the well-known perfumer and manufacturer of cosmetics, Richard Hudnut. In her picture she made clever fun of the agonies women undergo, the time and money they spend in beauty parlors.

Since she was almost totally devoid of a sense of humor, it was strange to me that Natacha Rambova was able to bring out so much excellent comedy. But this failure in humor was also shared by Rudolph. He was merry, childishly intrigued by simple pleasures. Nevertheless he seldom smiled, and more rarely laughed. It will be remembered that seldom upon the screen has Valentino smiled. This reticence on his part enabled his

Valentino as I Knew Him

smile to appear something very choice and precious. One felt flattered when one said or did anything to make him smile. The photographs of these two people almost invariably portray other emotions.

Valentino had not the slightest makings of a comedian. He never did anything funny in private life; he was not a practical joker, nor did he enjoy tricks. When he smiled it was almost invariably a smile of kindliness, such a smile for instance as one would bestow upon a child or an animal.

When he played with his dogs, or caressed his horses, or romped with children, he seldom laughed. Nor did he indulge in sneers or sarcasms. His temper was volcanic, but its exhibition was soon over; and it was then that he would smile. Invective he used, epithets, foul names and profanity; but among men only. He was punctilious in his language before women. In very truth, his entire intercourse with women was a subtle flattery which seemed to blanket every one with whom he came in contact.

Chapter 9

It must be admitted that the publicity department of every motion picture is allowed great leeway. It faces the arduous necessity to write readable stuff about the stars, and to see that it is published. For this reason, literally tons of material are published which frequently cause agonized cries from those written about, containing as it does more or less of truth, gawdily embroidered.

In this volume, however, I am endeavoring to depict Rudolph Valentino as he really was, and not to gild the lily; nor to build up, out of my desire, a monument in print of my hero that those who loved him or those who hated, if there truly were any, could complain of.

Stories of Valentino were conspicuously easy to place, so much so as to cause comment. But this only went to show that his picturesque personality made good copy. Newspapers are proverbially hard-boiled, and there is nowhere on record the existence of one easy enough to print out of friendship material it neither liked nor wanted. Therefore, it is only fair to suppose that the quantity of publicity concerning Valentino which the press

Valentino as I Knew Him

published, and the public absorbed, was considered to be of sufficient interest to give it the place of prominence it unfailingly enjoyed.

For another thing, I observed that whenever Valentino was interviewed, and I read the interview in the paper the next day, I discovered that he had said something of genuine interest. This is truly a mark of great showmanship, for, mark you, he never talked about himself unless directly questioned. Then he would reply with a becoming show of modesty, which possibly he may have felt.

He would generally begin to talk about some one thing in his marvelous collections. He never jumped from one subject to another, like a mental grasshopper nibbling here and there at various subjects, but he exercised the good taste to discourse intelligently upon one thing. Take, for example, his books. He possessed specimens which would grace museums, ancient vellum, marvelous examples of the engraver's art, gorgeous illustrations and beautiful specimens of the book-binder's craft; he had selected judiciously. These books were of a sort to intrigue even a connoisseur, nor were they above the intelligence of the lay mind. They were in Latin, French, German, Spanish, Italian, Old English, Russian, and Greek, and, with the exception of the books in these last two

A wall in the library of "Falcon Lair," indicating wide diversity of Valentino's intellectual tastes

by S. George Ullman

languages, Valentino was familiar with the contents of all of them. I may misjudge him, he may have known even these.

His library was not large. I should even call it small, but very distinguished. He seldom bought sets of books, no matter how valuable. To be sure he had a few, such as Balzac, Dickens, Tolstoi; but the anthologies, collections of wit and humor, speeches of eminent men, which every *bourgeois* library contains, were conspicuously absent from that of Rudolph Valentino.

He was so keen on costumes of every nationality and every period that many of his most expensive books were on these subjects, gorgeously colored plates. Of almost equal importance to Rudy were books on the customs of nations, their habits and amusements; and with these he was intimately acquainted. It is my belief that you could not open a conversation about any race, even down to nomadic bands, about which Valentino would not know something. And very often his knowledge and marvelous memory would astound you.

As so many of his pictures, both produced and projected, dealt with historical subjects, it was necessary for him to know history, and this he did.

In order to obtain all the information possible, he generally read history in two languages, that

Valentino as I Knew Him

of its own country, and English. In this way it became so impressed upon his mind that he was not obliged to memorize. Two readings in two languages were sufficient.

This would frequently amaze reporters, who generally expected to find movie stars beautiful but dumb.

If a reporter showed any interest in the armor or firearms of which the Valentino collection is *sui generis*, here once more his showmanship came into evidence. Not only did he possess specimens of every sort of sword, cuirass, spear, dart, javelin, assegai and what not, but firearms from the most ancient make down to the latest Colt were his. And if you thought that the carving upon an ancient sword-blade was inexplicable or unknown to Rudolph Valentino, all you had to do to correct your impression was to question him.

With a flow of words in the careful English which many foreigners acquire, he would explain to you, not only the carving's significance, but, in all probability, an historical sketch of the man who made it.

And, again, his was no cluttered collection. Small, distinctive, carefully chosen, exquisitely placed, his groups, upon red velvet backgrounds, were restful to the eye and intriguing to the imagination.

by S. George Ullman

He had no large pieces of statuary, but delicate examples of Tanagra, carved ivory, old silver, jade and onyx were scattered not more than one or two in a room, so that each had a dignified space in which to display its beauty.

Knowing the history of each of these bibelots, it can easily be seen that Valentino had plenty with which to interest reporters of both sexes, and one never left his house without a definite story which was very well worth printing. Generally, it may be said that, no matter how prejudiced these feature writers were before meeting Valentino, they invariably left his presence with a very healthy respect for him as a man. If they came to scoff, they remained to praise.

Rudy was always courteous to people of the press, particularly to women. If unable to keep an appointment he would select some unusual way in which to recompense the caller for loss of time. If it were a man, a box of cigars or some of his imported cigarettes made interesting by his monogram, or, if a woman, seldom anything as commonplace as flowers. On one occasion I recall he sent a woman writer a bottle of choice perfume; written on the card were the words, "I will say it with perfume, it lasts longer." His cards, by the way, were of parchment.

Chapter 10

During this period the Valentinos were living in the house on Whitley Heights which Rudy had occupied as a bachelor. This was only about ten minutes' drive from the studio; they were enabled to run back and forth at will.

From its windows you could see the hills which form the Hollywood Bowl, and the flaming cross which marked The Pilgrimage Play.

It was a hillside house. You entered a hall which gave upon a floor with only two bedrooms and two baths. You had to go downstairs to find the living room, with its black marble floor and cerise hangings. The color scheme of the bedrooms was canary and black, the exotic combinations of the entire house being the work of Natacha. It was Oriental in the extreme and its violent contrasts of color were anything but restful. Up a few steps, at one end of the living room, was the dining room, which was quite small, so small indeed that not more than eight persons could sit at table. The furniture was Chinese red lacquer, with black satin upholstery. This room was sepa-

Valentino as I Knew Him

rated from the living room only by an iron railing covered with black velvet.

Midway in the living room was an enormous bay window on the deeply cushioned seat of which four or five persons could sit with ease. It was here that I had many happy evenings with the Valentinos discussing the homely things of life.

Few people know that Rudolph Valentino was a poet and philosopher. His book of poems, entitled *Day Dreams*, is published both in England and America, and contains such gems of thought that I am constrained to quote one or two of them here:

A BABY'S SKIN

Texture of a butterfly's wing,
Colored like a dawned rose,
Whose perfume is the breath of God.
Such is the web wherein is held
The treasure of the treasure chest,
The priceless gift—the Child of Love.

THREE GENERATIONS OF KISSES

A Mother's kisses
Are blessed with love
Straight from the heart
Of Heaven above.

Valentino as I Knew Him

Love's benediction
Her dear caress,
The sum of all our happiness.

Till we kiss the lips
Of the mate of our soul
We never know Love
Has reached its goal.
Caress divine,
You reign until
A baby's kiss seems sweeter still.

That beloved blossom
A baby's face
Seems to be
Love's resting place.
And a million kisses
Tenderly
Linger there in ecstasy.

Were I told to select
Just one kiss a day,
Oh, what a puzzle!
I would say.
Still a baby's kiss
I'd choose, you see,
For in that wise choice
I'd gain All Three.

by S. George Ullman

These two seem to me to prove the delicacy of Rudolph Valentino's imagination. He crystallizes his love of the children he dreamed of but never possessed. He often spoke of the time when babies would be in their home, and one of the most poignant griefs in my memories of my friend are that he never realized this supreme desire.

Natacha was not opposed to having children, although this calumny has frequently been published about her. She only said that she thought it was wisdom for Rudy to complete his career before they had them, because no one in the motion picture business could be the proper sort of parent while living the abnormal life a star is obliged to live. She always declared that when they ceased making pictures she was perfectly willing and very anxious to have children.

We often discussed these things while sitting in the big window seat. Doubtless here was born many a rhyme which later took form in his book of poems, *Day Dreams.*

As I thumb the little volume, I find one more impassioned verse so significant of the great lover of the screen that I am fain to quote it.

If, while reading these lines, you will visualize the scene in the bridal chamber of *The Sainted Devil,* in which he draws near to his bride for his

Valentino as I Knew Him

nuptial kiss, you will realize the thoughts which were in his mind at that moment:

YOU

*You are the History of Love and
its Justification.
The Symbol of Devotion.
The Blessedness of Womanhood.
The Incentive of Chivalry.
The Reality of Ideals.
The Verity of Joy.
Idolatry's Defense.
The Proof of Goodness.
The Power of Gentleness.
Beauty's Acknowledgment.
Vanity's Excuse.
The Promise of Truth.
The Melody of Life.
The Caress of Romance.
The Dream of Desire.
The Sympathy of Understanding.
My Heart's Home.
The Proof of Faith.
Sanctuary of my Soul.
My Belief of Heaven.
Eternity of all Happiness.
My Prayers.
You.*

by S. George Ullman

Considering the brevity of his own tragic life, the following bit of profound philosophy strikes me as prophetic:

DUST TO DUST

I take a bone—I gaze at it in wonder—You, O bit of strength that was. In you to-day I see the whited sepulcher of nothingness—but you were the shaft that held the wagon of Life. Your strength held together the vehicle of Man until God called and the Soul answered.

Flickering glimpses of the finished beauty of these thoughts I frequently discovered in these wonderful discussions on the philosophy of life, its beauty, its sadness, its unclaimed joys, at which time I discovered rare beauties in the souls of both.

Chapter 11

BECAUSE of the childlike joy with which the Valentinos threw themselves into preparation for their first Christmas together in California, I almost came to think that they believed in Santa Claus.

Naturally I expected each to give a gift to the other, and a very handsome one. But I had no idea that I would be pulled hither and yon, called to confer secretly, first with one and then with the other, until my mind was in a whirl.

Considering the fact that serious differences between these two had begun to manifest themselves, this Christmas enthusiasm gave me great satisfaction. I could not believe that the trouble was basic when both husband and wife were perfectly serious and eager in their desire to please each other supremely.

Receiving an imperative summons from Natacha to come at once because Rudy was out, I dashed up to the house, fearing the worst, only to find that I was to carry out for her an idea which has since caused more comment than any gift from a woman to a man she loved since the days of Cleopatra and Marc Antony. It was the famous platinum slave

Valentino as I Knew Him

bracelet which the world has attributed as the gift of no less than a score of beautiful women, but which in reality was a Christmas present from his own wife, and was made to order from a design which she herself drew and gave to me to carry out.

For obvious reasons, I have kept silent when confronted with divers rumors, but now that the world is learning for the first time the true Valentino in all his weaknesses, his strength, his fascination, and the respect he inspired among the men and women who knew him best, I am telling the truth about the famous slave bracelet.

It was given to Rudy by Natacha.

When newspaper writers, intent upon earning their salaries on space, discovered the innocent fact that Rudolph Valentino wore a slave bracelet, and worried it as a dog worries a bone, dragging its description and their deductions concerning it from paragraph to paragraph, it is worthy of note that their jibes and insults never for one moment tempted Valentino to leave off wearing it. That this shows courage of a supreme order no man can deny, for fear of ridicule is an inherent quality in most mortals. Calamities can be borne with more fortitude than ridicule, and severe pain with more equanimity than continuous gnat bites. But

Valentino as I Knew Him

Valentino was superbly indifferent to both. When he set his feet on a certain path, he pursued it calmly to the end, fixing his mind upon his destination and disregarding both rocks and pebbles which might cause him to stumble. A quality of greatness, I call this serene, uplifted attitude.

Nor could a husband's fidelity to the gift of his wife, prepared with such loving care, be attributed to stubbornness. To my mind it is an insult to the quality of Rudy's love for Natacha to suggest such a thing. I am inclined to call it more a quality of faithfulness to memories of the greatest happiness which ever came into his life, that he persisted in wearing this much discussed slave bracelet, and wore it to his death.

The slave bracelet given Rudolph Valentino by Natacha Rambova rests with him still in his tomb.

And the New York reporter who, in commenting on the unfortunate editorial published in a Chicago newspaper, quoted Rudy as saying, "Yes, I shall continue to wear this bracelet, as it was given to me by some one whom I dearly love," remarked that then Valentino looked thoughtfully down at the bracelet and off into space, caught, to my mind, more nearly the truth of Valentino's feelings in regard to the bracelet, than any other writer who commented upon it. Every time that Rudy's eyes rested upon his slave bracelet I be-

by S. George Ullman

lieve that the image of his wife rose before his mental vision.

Rudy's Christmas gift to Natacha had a history which can be duplicated in the memories of countless young couples.

This is the story of it.

Several years before, when Rudy and Natacha were engaged; and, by the way, it was the year before his divorce from Jean Acker became final; they were looking at a watch surrounded by diamonds, and embedded in a thinly cut moonstone. It could be worn as locket or watch; but, at that time, the price of $2,000 was more than Rudy could afford.

Natacha had been crazy about it and had always remembered it, once in a while referring to its chaste beauty.

Evidently Valentino had borne this in mind for, on another morning, I was hastily summoned to his bungalow dressing room. With suppressed excitement, he seized my arm and asked me if I remembered the times when Natacha had described this watch.

I did not, but I lied and said I did, for it seemed impossible to dampen in any way Rudy's ardor. Feverishly he gave me the name of the jeweler, refreshed my mind by a careful and minute description of the bauble, and urged me to go down

Valentino as I Knew Him

that very moment and buy it if it was still obtainable.

I went to the bank and drew two one thousand dollar bills. One I placed in my wallet, and the other I held in my hand.

I had no difficulty in finding it, for the moment I began to describe the watch the salesman interrupted me, saying that he knew exactly the one I meant.

Owing to the fact that it was still on their hands I imagined they might be willing to take less. I therefore laid the thousand dollar bill on the counter and offered to take the watch at that price.

After some demur, a few impassioned arguments, and the statement that at this price it was nothing short of a gift, I succeeded in purchasing the moonstone watch at exactly one-half what had been asked the Valentinos some years before.

Evidently the sight of a thousand dollar bill was too much for them.

On the way home I stopped at the bank, placed the remaining thousand dollar bill to Valentino's account and came home in triumph to my friend, who was delighted with a business ability which he never would have thought of emulating for himself.

While driving along, with this precious jewel, in its white velvet box, safe in my pocket, I could

by S. George Ullman

not help thinking of the thousands of young people, either engaged or married, who window-shopped in their spare moments, and selected their heart's desires behind plate glass with an "Oh, I wish we could afford that!" from the girl, followed by an equally impassioned "Well, darling, just as soon as I get that raise from The Old Man, you shall have it."

Paralleled in ten thousand lesser ways was the window-shopping of the Valentinos. Yet I dare say that just as much love and generosity were in their gifts to each other, as in the humblest lad's selection of a silver plated premium for his sweetheart, to be paid for by coupons.

From this time on, seeing that I was to partake of a Christmas the like of which I had not seen for twenty years, I threw myself into their plans with all the enthusiasm of which I was capable. Dark secrets were in the air every moment. Whenever one or the other would be alone I was sure to receive a summons for a conference, and, by their laughter and air of mystery, I rather imagined that I too was due for a surprise.

Now Christmas in California is a feature which I have never encountered elsewhere. What Californians call cold weather is about the climate we Easterners find in autumn, in what we call Indian summer, with the exception that, there having

Valentino as I Knew Him

been no frost, autumn colors are lacking. I refer merely to the quality of the atmosphere, for that which meets the eye is very different.

The hills, green in summer, have now turned dun. The grass on the lawns is still green, the roses are still in bloom, and the flowering shrubs lend splotches of color to a landscape of a beauty to be found nowhere else but the southlands of Europe.

The so-called rainy season has not yet begun, and Christmas may always be counted upon to be a day of fair weather.

Present-giving on Christmas in California overflows the boundaries of families and spreads itself delightfully among friends and choice acquaintances. It is safe to say that on Christmas morning almost every one goes out for an hour or two to distribute gifts of remembrance in person. It reminded me more of the old-fashioned habit of New Year calls than anything I could remember.

On this particular Christmas, at six o'clock in the morning I was called from my bed by the frantic ringing of the telephone. Answering it, I found myself commanded, after a cheery "Merry Christmas," to bring Mrs. Ullman and my little boy Danny, then about six years old, and come immediately to the Valentino home. It was Na-

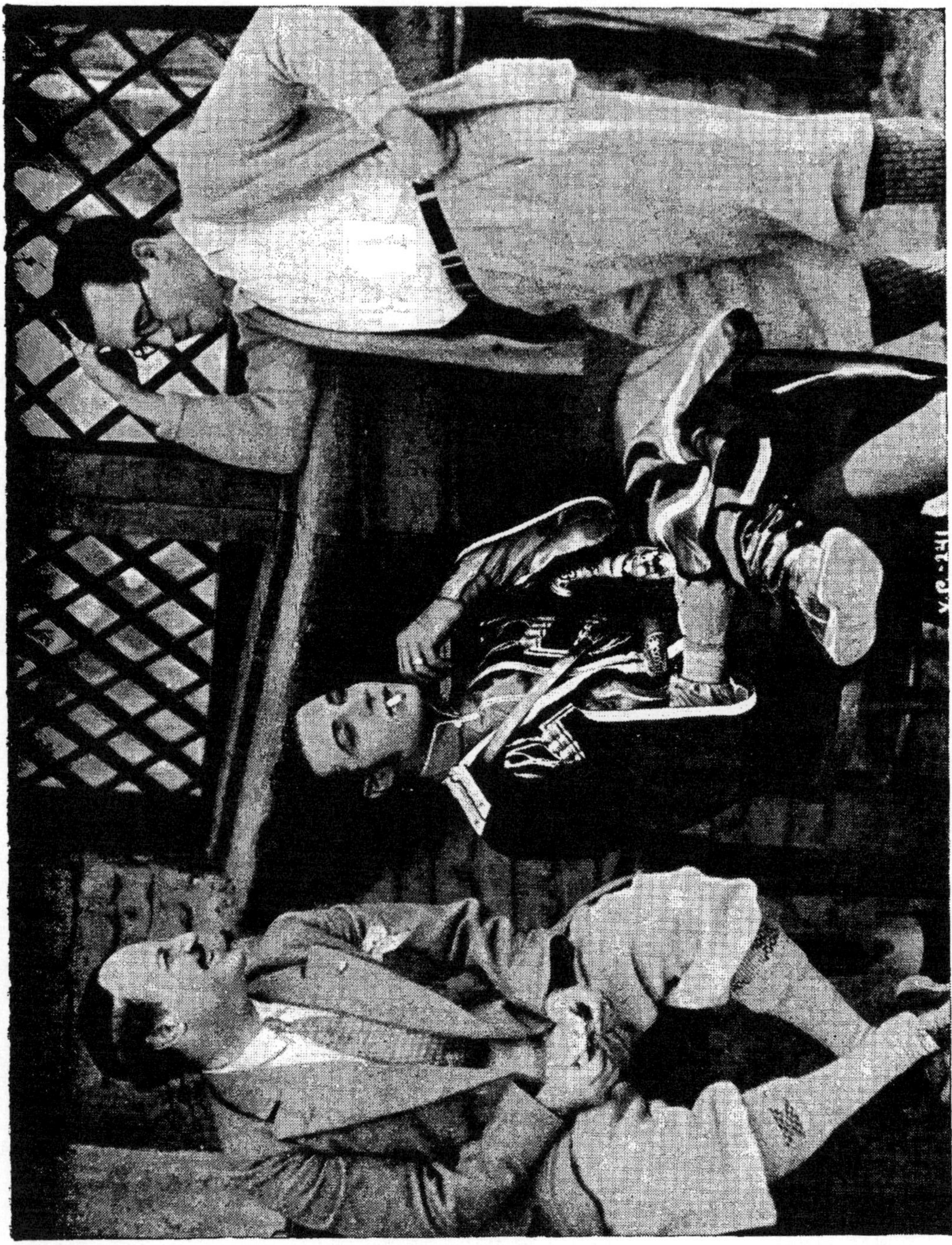

by S. George Ullman

tacha's voice, and she told me explicitly not to stop for breakfast, but to come at once.

Scrambling into our clothes, we hurriedly obeyed. Our own excitement almost equaled that of our small boy, who was fairly dancing with impatience to get to his beloved "Uncle Rudy."

Upon our arrival there, not later than seven o'clock, we were met in the patio by Natacha, who halted us with a great air of mystery and would not permit us to enter.

When Natacha chose to exert herself, she could be the most entertaining woman I have ever met, and she chose to exert herself that Christmas morning, when, without even a cup of coffee, we had dashed around to obey her summons. It was perhaps half an hour she held us there in the bright California sunshine, curbing our impatience with what grace we could. Then, a wild shout of "All ready!" was heard from within the house and, leading the way, Mrs. Valentino hurried us down the stairs into the living room where a sight met our eyes to take the breath of grown-ups, let alone of an impressionable child like Danny.

Covering the entire black marble floor of the great living room was a network of railroad tracks, tunnels, roundhouses, electric switches, freight cars, passenger cars, engines and what not, the

Valentino as I Knew Him

whole appearing as a railway terminal in a great city might look to an aviator flying over it.

The cost of this extravagant toy I dared not estimate, and Natacha told us that all night, in fact until dawn, Rudy had spent his time setting up this toy, catching a terrible cold from sitting and crawling around on the cold marble floor for so many hours.

But his joy in seeing the excitement of Danny as the mysterious electricity caused these tiny trains to move forward and back, to switch around, more than compensated Rudy for all his toil and trouble. Natacha jeered at him in a friendly way and declared that Rudy set the toy up as much to enjoy himself as to please the child.

Possibly this was true, as I myself had guilty recollections of doing similar things in taking my small son to a circus I had a sneaking desire to see myself.

I was reminded also of Rudy's passion for machinery and his love for taking things apart, "To see the wheels go wound," as Helen's babies used to say.

I remember that at one time he overhauled his expensive Voisin car with the help of his chauffeur, who was an expert mechanician, cleaned and oiled every part, and put it back again. This he did, I am persuaded, from an intense curiosity to see

by S. George Ullman

how the thing worked. He could not bear to be in ignorance of the source of its power, yet at the same time he had a mechanic's delight in tinkering and fooling with machinery.

Breakfast was rather a sketchy meal, for over in the corner, shrouded under sheets, stood what even Danny knew to be a Christmas tree. When this was unveiled, it turned out to be a very gorgeous thing, hung with many presents, not only for us, but for the friends who were expected to drop in during the day.

The night before, Natacha told us, she and Rudy had had a quarrel, and in the early morning they were hardly speaking. But I observed that the good cheer and friendliness engendered by the Christmas season had evidently completely wiped away all differences, and they were as tender and loving to each other as I had ever seen them.

After this, came the presentation of the Valentino gifts to each other. With real solemnity I saw Natacha place the now famous slave bracelet on Rudy's wrist, from which it was never removed, and witnessed his kiss of fervent gratitude for the symbolism it expressed. He declared that he was the slave of her beauty and kindliness, and Natacha seemed to welcome the expressions of fervent gratitude which he uttered.

When she opened the white velvet case and

Valentino as I Knew Him

saw the coveted jewel she uttered a cry of genuine pleasure and flung herself into his arms with the abandonment of love.

Rudy was enchanted by Natacha's delight. She immediately put the watch on and continued to admire it all day, and always, and her delight indicated a far greater pleasure than in any gift he could have received for himself. Nothing ever gave him such pleasure as to make his wife happy, and in this he exercised an ingenuity and persistence which made him one of the great lovers of the earth in real life.

Chapter 12

WHAT PRICE BEAUTY ought to be called The Divorce Picture, as the difficulties which arose from its inception to its close covered precisely the time of the differences between the Valentinos.

Not that I would have you understand that the difficulties about the pictures were the only things that led to the divorce. It is my opinion that, when her dictatorship was taken from her, it was not long before her loyalty to Valentino, not only to his business interests, but to him as a wife, began to fail her.

When she ceased to collaborate, she also failed to coöperate with him in more ways than one; and a man as proud and sensitive as Valentino could not fail to detect her failing interest and to feel a profound hurt, a hurt so deep and poignant that he carried it with him to his grave.

From a passionate interest in his future and a desire to promote his best interests, Rudy now began to observe that her fancy was straying into other paths and fastening itself to other objects and interests. A natural coldness now began to appear, which threw Natacha more and more upon her own resources. It caused her husband the most profound anguish, not only hurting, as it did, his natural male vanity, but injuring him in his deepest soul. He felt for the first time that his love was not appreciated, and he began to suspect that he had been married, not for himself alone, but partly as a means to an end. That end was, first and foremost, Natacha's overpowering, unalterable determination to be a figure which the motion picture world could not ignore. That she aspired to take first place as a director and producer of super-pictures is not, in my opinion, too great an ambition to lay at her door.

Cleopatra is her greatest prototype in history. In fact, if I believed in reincarnation, I could very easily imagine that the soul of Natacha Rambova, with all of her physical perfections and her mysterious fascination, had once inhabited the body of Egypt's queen. And that the Nile and its desert sands had once been her natural habitat.

That Natacha yielded to this overpowering urge of ambition must not be held against her by the analyst, for, from her earliest childhood, traits which indicated this desire to be preëminent cropped out whenever the smallest opening appeared. Vital, dynamic, and capable of long stretches of work which were surprising in one of such delicate physique; these were qualities which

by S. George Ullman

never could have been entirely stifled without wrecking her. She was the victim of her own ambition, which, in my opinion, was congenital. Nor has the world heard the last of her. Such genius will sooner or later discover its *metier*, and it would not surprise me in the slightest to discover one day that Natacha Rambova has completed a masterpiece in some line of artistry to compel the attention of a discriminating world.

For one reason, she was never afraid of poverty, nor hardship. She would starve to accomplish an ideal. Her soul was above taking cognizance of bodily discomfort. On the other hand, Rudy, while also an artist, would never have endured rags or dirt, hunger or cold, to win heaven itself. Valentino was a sybarite, a Lucullus, a Brillat-Savarin, and no epicure nor one born with epicurean tastes could ever be so basically a genius as to be willing to go through a hell of deprivation, even to win that preëminence which he most ardently craved. For this reason I do not hesitate to assert that, while Natacha Rambova could never cause a world-worship such as Rudy achieved almost without effort, yet Natacha was the greater soul. And it is only fair to say that her culture, which she painstakingly but subtly communicated to her husband, was one which others recognized and which in my opinion put him forever in her debt. He was truly, and in the highest sense, elevated by his association with Natacha.

Nevertheless, she was sped in her labor of love by the fact that inherently Rudy possessed a fineness and gentleness and chivalry which formed a superb foundation for her superstructure of culture. An example was his regret when the divorce occurred. I remember that he said to me:

"You know I bear Natacha no grudge, and I wish her all the success in the world. She'll get it, too, for she is still young and has her life before her. I am so glad that I did not rob her of the best years of her life. If the separation had to come, I am glad that it came so quickly."

I knew he felt himself deeply injured. I consider this a rather fine thing for him to say, especially as I realize that he meant it, and was not saying it for effect.

In fact, I have no recollection of ever having seen Valentino do anything for effect. All his friends will tell you that he was ever supremely natural. He never posed, nor struck an attitude, nor made an attempt to appear what he was not. He was one man who must have been a hero to his valet.

I take it that this was due to the fact that he could not imagine any one really disliking him. He had the unfailing confidence of a collie pup,

by S. George Ullman

a pretty baby, or a toddling two-year-old, who staggers to your knee and looks up into your eyes with no knowledge of your ability to strike.

To be colloquial, I never in my life saw Rudolph Valentino "strut his stuff."

Conceit or egotism as we know it in other men and women was surprisingly lacking in Rudy. It was more than that. Conceit, I take it, is an attribute of an inferior mind or personality, whereas Rudy's paramount confidence in himself, a quality which has no tangible existence nor name, was individuality raised to the *nth* power. I have been about a bit, have traveled some and am no longer a callow youth, yet I can say that I never met so engaging and captivating a personality as Valentino's. And the fact that he expected you to see him as he knew he was, and as he wanted you to see him, formed the basis of this amazing form of self-confidence. If I may be allowed a poetic flight in which I seldom indulge, I say that Valentino bloomed like a gorgeous flower, and with no desire to be self-conscious. For example, an American Beauty rose just blooms, with no expectation of being either liked or disliked; it just is, and that's all. So with Valentino.

I do not deny that there was a great deal of secret jealousy of Rudy among men who were slightly acquainted with him. I think it never

Valentino as I Knew Him

existed among his close friends, although I do not see how so gorgeous a personality, sweeping all before it, could fail to cause an occasional twinge, even among his intimates. But if this occurred, it was instantly dispelled at Rudy's approach, before which everything unkind, resentful or hateful disappeared like magic.

He caused occasional discomfort among his associates in the studio by his preoccupied manner. I have frequently seen him walk about with his eyes fixed on space, ignoring the morning salutation or the greeting which every one has a right to expect. He never knew that he was thus slighting those admirers who valued his recognition as something very precious. If he had he would have wrenched his mind away from its absorption, even at the risk of the loss of his continuity of thought, in order not to offend. He was truly one of the most courteous and kindly of mortals.

But he was also a dreamer. A bit of blue sky, the flight of a swallow, the iridescence of a butterfly's wing, a strange perfume or a strain of exotic music would snatch at his imagination, which, once loosed, would drench his soul in a secret beauty which he confided to no one. And this detachment masqueraded as a self-absorption which certain of his friends resented. For my own

by S. George Ullman

part, I rather respected these retreats into himself, for I observed that out of them always came something worth while. Had we ever accused Rudy of these things which I am now writing, and which he never would have admitted to be true, he would have been as shy and sheepish and gauche as a school-boy caught in his first exhibit of puppy love. Certain secrets of his soul Valentino preferred to keep his own. Thus analyzing what I only came to know through close observation of my friend seems in a way to be somewhat indelicate, not to say indecent. For I am probing into the holy of holies of a human soul.

I must be excused, if I do merit blame in this matter, by the necessity to impart to the world the intimate knowledge of Valentino which I shared with few.

Chapter 13

IF you visualize the type of woman, gray-haired, motherly, up to date in a sane way, yet one whom one called "Auntie" as soon as acquaintance would permit, you have before you the beautiful character of Mrs. Teresa Werner, whose mention in the will of Valentino as sharing equally with his brother and sister, caused a wave of astonishment to run over the civilized world.

Knowing her and the impartial, tactful, kindly part she played in the growing coolness between these two, which she and I both saw was tending toward a separation, if not a divorce, I was not surprised. In drawing his last will, Rudy insisted on remembering her generously, for he experienced a passionate gratitude toward one who, while naturally tending toward a defense of her own niece, yet was able to see his side of the question, and to persuade Natacha to a lenience and compassionate patience which, if it had lasted, would have healed the breach.

There are no words to describe the part Mrs. Werner played during this troublous period. It is trite to say that she was like oil on the troubled

Valentino as I Knew Him

waters; yet no other simile is so felicitous. When the waves of their discussions ran high and dashed themselves upon the rocks of their own personalities, along would come Auntie with a healing touch here and tender word there, to smooth the wrinkles from the quarrelers' brows, and even, not infrequently, to cause a temporary truce to be signed. After a furious argument, including recrimination of the most biting and personal sort, I have seen Auntie cause them to kiss each other in an effort to retain that love which we all knew, in our secret hearts, was receding fast.

Sad indeed were those days to all of us. For nothing is more tragic than to be present at the death-bed of love.

Rudy flung himself into the making of *The Eagle* hoping that he would have neither time nor opportunity to think.

Natacha, having completed *What Price Beauty,* took to making long trips with her car, going no one knew where, often staying two days. This we believed to be an effort to distract her mind from her troubles with Rudy, to make certain decisions and to arrive at final conclusions.

That the decisions she finally arrived at were erroneous and tended only to widen the breach between the two, is one of the most regrettable things which could possibly have occurred at just

Valentino as I Knew Him

this time. Arguments and loving remonstrances were of no avail. She had her own codes and standards of life, and these she believed to be nobody's business but her own.

Any one knowing the situation can imagine how just and righteous were the ministrations of her aunt, Mrs. Werner, at this time. She soothed Rudy's just resentment, endeavoring to palliate Natacha's conduct, at the same time endeavoring to bring the young wife back to a realization of the duty and respect which she felt her niece owed to her husband. That she acomplished this without irritating either party, and retained the devotion of both, is ample reason why she occupies today the position of an ambassador whose reward is earned.

For my own part, I do not begrudge her the share in Rudy's estate which she is to enjoy. It was what he wanted to do for the woman who played the part of mother to his soul in its loneliest and most desolate hour.

Had his own mother been at hand, I doubt if she could have proved as efficacious and wise in this crucial period as did Auntie. For having seen the brother, who made an extended visit to Rudy just before his death, and whose return has given me a wider opportunity to analyze his mind and understand his character, I make bold to say that

by S. George Ullman

Auntie's understanding heart did what his own mother could not.

The same condition obtained in the Guglielmi family which many of us have observed here in America: into a family of owls an eaglet is born. The owls look wise, but their wisdom will not bear the test. The eaglet longs to soar. The owls have no strength to their wings, and therefore they gossip among themselves as to the strange and inexplicable tendencies of their eagle-child to fly into unknown ways.

Such families are always in desperate fear of what their eagle-child will do to smirch the family name of Owl. Newspaper headlines, the disapproving comments of neighbors, even the barred gates of jail are forever in the background of these dull and unimaginative minds. From the story of the early life which Rudy has many a time told me, I have formed a picture of his *bourgeois* family. His mother has expressed herself as being forever afraid of what Rodolfo would do. To her, it was a never ending shame that he was expelled from school when he played hookey. But it was to *see a King!* And, to accomplish that, Rudy would have risked dismissal from a hundred schools and laughed to realize that he had accomplished what he set out to do.

Valentino as I Knew Him

Kings are interesting folk, and well worth a sacrifice on the part of a common mortal.

Valentino was never sordid. His escapades from his early youth, up to his tragic death, were always of a gay and gallant nature, and he laughed at danger.

Beltram Masses, the famous Spanish court painter, Rudy had known in Europe. He came to Hollywood for the express purpose of painting Valentino, and in the hope that he would obtain other commissions among the movie stars, which he succeeded in doing. Marion Davies was the first and most important of these.

An impressive exhibition of the work of Beltram Masses was given at the Ambassador Hotel in Los Angeles; for two weeks it drew crowds. It was to be observed that the portraits of Marion Davies and Rudolph Valentino attracted more attention than those of all the court beauties this famous artist had painted. I think I have never seen a more beautiful portrait of a woman than Beltram Masses succeeded in doing of Miss Davies. He caught that look of innocence which in her pictures is one of her greatest assets. In his two portraits of Valentino he caught the air of gay defiance and laughing chivalry of the courtier cavalier. The portrait Beltram Masses did of Valentino as *Julio* in *The Four Horsemen of the*

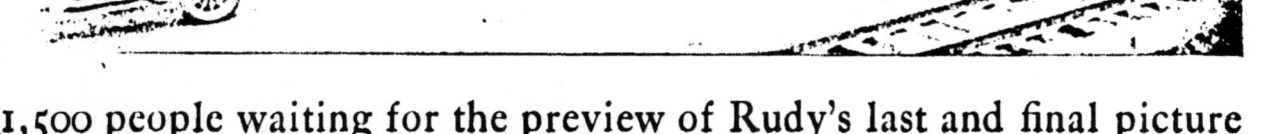

1,500 people waiting for the preview of Rudy's last and final picture

by S. George Ullman

Apocalypse is the one which Pola Negri so desires that the heirs of the Valentino estate shall give to her.

Beltram Masses, in his character of intimate friend, also endeavored to bridge the trouble between the Valentinos, and prevent the impending separation. For he feared, as we all did, that, if they ever separated, a divorce would follow. Both were proud, difficult to manage, and with that tremendous sense of ego which seems to render compromise well nigh impossible.

But to no avail.

The occurrence which was one of the few open examples people had of the disharmony between these two, happened in this wise.

Miss Davies and Valentino, feeling that the superb portraits Beltram Masses had painted of them deserved more than the mere financial remuneration, decided to give an elaborate private reception which should introduce the artist to their choicest friends. At this time, also, the three portraits were to be exhibited, and given opportunity for more minute examination.

Unfortunately, however, because the suggestion came from these two, and was later presented to Mrs. Valentino for her coöperation and approval, she of course to be co-hostess at the function, she became so indignant because the idea had not originated with her, that she prevented her husband from appearing at the proper time. She refused to dress. Finally Rudy caused her to appreciate how rude their behavior would be if they continued to absent themselves from their own reception; whereupon Natacha yielded, and at a very late hour, the Valentinos appeared, greeted their guests and immediately left for home, abandoning their guests to their own resources.

The fact that this breach of etiquette was wholly foreign to Valentino's nature, and also repugnant to him, could not fail to become known to all his friends. But that did not prevent the elite of Los Angeles, who had been bid to the reception, from feeling righteously indignant at being flouted by "mere movie stars", God save the mark.

Beltram Masses, knowing as he did the state of affairs in the Valentino family, was possibly the only one present who knew without any explanation what had caused this apparent neglect.

About this time, the purchase of the handsome new house in Beverly Hills was consummated. For some time it had been Natacha's desire to live in this exclusive and more fashionable district; and, even though Rudy knew that a separation

by S. George Ullman

was imminent, he concluded the purchase and Falcon Lair became his.

This may have indicated that up to the very last Rudy hoped that the differences could be adjusted, and that Natacha could grace this gorgeous hillside home in which she so ardently desired to shine.

Be that as it may, the fact remains that Natacha never spent one night under its roof.

Despite the efforts of both the Valentinos to keep their differences out of the newspapers, the situation had become so tense that news of it began to filter through the guards, and newspaper men began to gather and question for news.

No matter how one tried to throw these persistent news-gatherers off the scent, it could not be done. They knew, and we knew that they knew that something was brewing. And, little by little, these stories crept into print.

Naturally, this caused gossip; and gossip caused more intense irritation to nerves already frayed by the friction of increasing marital differences. Finally Natacha declared her intention of going to New York.

Rudy was agreeable to this, but amended her decision by urging her to go directly to her mother at Nice, hoping not only that a separation from him would be beneficial, but that the good advice he knew she would receive from her mother might influence her.

At any rate, he knew that, away from him, and with time to reflect, she could not fail to find herself; and this, no matter which way it cut, was what Rudy chivalrously desired.

I being called East on business about this time, and Natacha being determined to go at once, Rudy decided to send Auntie with her, knowing well that in her he was sending an envoy and ambassador upon whose wisdom he depended with wholehearted fervor.

These plans were thrown open to the press, and on the morning that we left a great crowd assembled at the station to see the travelers off. Rudolph and Natacha were driven down in their big Isotta-Fraschini town car, and were greeted by the clicks of countless cameras.

It was part of our program of endeavoring to conceal the fact that we feared a divorce, to have Rudy and Natacha pose for that final kiss which appeared in so many newspapers. I am not aware how Natacha felt, whether she was genuinely sorry to part from her husband, or whether at this time it was a genuine relief. As for the feelings of Rudy, no one could fail to see that his heart was torn with grief, for despite the prevalent superstition that a man should never watch a beloved

by S. George Ullman

woman out of his sight for fear he may never see her again, Rudy either ignored or forgot this stricture, for he clung to the steps of the observation car as long as he dared and then ran along the platform beside the slowly moving train which he feared was bearing her out of his sight forever; which afterwards proved to be true.

As the long train gained momentum and began to move more rapidly, Natacha Rambova had the satisfaction of seeing in the eyes of her husband that expression of love and great yearning which so many times we have seen in his acting upon the screen. This time, being a witness to its reality, I unhestitatingly declare that only because Valentino was so great a lover in real life could he ever have become the greatest lover of the screen.

Never have I seen greater anguish, nor more poignant tenderness expressed on a human countenance, and this picture of Valentino was constantly coming into my mind during those days when he fought for his life so valiantly, and when I knew his thoughts were turning more and more to Natacha.

Natacha and Auntie occupied a drawing room where their meals were served, and where I joined them, often spending part of the afternoon in their company.

At all times, when it was feasible, Mrs. Werner

used her gentle arguments to persuade her niece to that compromise without which no married couples can hope to live harmoniously.

Natacha, always diplomatic, put up no counter arguments; but her iron determination to carry out her own career became known when we arrived in New York and she flatly refused to go to her mother, even though we urged upon her that her husband would join her there as soon as his picture was finished.

The deaf ear Natacha turned upon us, in spite of our best efforts, proved to my mind that from the first she had had no intentions of leaving New York. At once she began to besiege me with requests to find an opening for her in pictures.

Pursuant to these plans she took an apartment at 9 West 81st Street, and set about making a home for herself, with Auntie as chaperon.

I do not mean to imply that Natacha had definitely given up all hope of a reconciliation, for I recall that one morning when I went out to see her, about ten o'clock, she appeared in a white negligée gorgeously embroidered in gold, with her luxuriant hair braided in two long loose braids, down her back, her face pale, her eyes delicately ringed from a sleepless night, and her whole attitude one of wan dejection.

I determined to question her definitely, to see if

by S. George Ullman

I could find out what she really thought, and what she purposed to do.

"Do you love Rudy?" I asked her.

Twisting her hands together, in a small voice she replied:

"I—I don't know!"

"Do you want to go back to him?"

"I—I don't know!"

"Do you want to get a divorce and lose Rudy out of your life forever?"

She paused at this, and stared at me with her great eyes full of woe.

"I—I don't—know!" she faltered. And then burst into a flood of tears. Whereupon I knew no more than when I began to question her. Nor, I am convinced, did she.

All during this time letters of more or less bitterness, recrimination and accusation, had been flying back and forth between Hollywood and New York, until finally one particular telegram was sent by Natacha which forever ended any possibility of a reconciliation.

Business now urgently calling me back to California, I turned Mrs. Valentino's interests over to a friend of mine, with instructions to serve her to the best of his ability.

That he did so, we have ample proof in the fact that he secured for her a contract to star in

Valentino as I Knew Him

a picture called *When Love Grows Cold,* a most fitting title considering the circumstances.

With the excuse of the necessity to purchase a wardrobe for this picture, Natacha went abroad, took the preliminary steps of establishing her residence in Paris in order to obtain a divorce, then paid a visit to her mother in Nice.

Then began caustic cables from Mrs. Hudnut, who, since she had heard but one side of the story, and did not possess her sister's breadth of character, keen imagination and vision, gave scant consideration to the story Valentino might possibly have to tell.

These messages cut Rudy to the heart, their tenor being so contrary to the oft-repeated statement that he was regarded more as an own son than as an in-law.

As soon as Natacha had left California, Rudy, in order to give himself no time to think, began to take painting lessons from Beltram-Masses, his friend; who, discovering a real talent in Valentino, did his best to develop it. They spent many hours in serious study; which, together with his work at the studio, gave him little time to himself.

Nevertheless, he began to take up once more the friends from whom he had been alienated by his marriage. Natacha was one of those women who could brook no interest in the heart of a man she loved but her own. She wished to reign supreme, and to this end she slowly but surely separated her husband from all his old companions.

Had it not been for these absorptions, it is my opinion that Valentino would have taken the first train possible and followed his wife to New York. But, after the reaction which that fatal telegram caused, his whole attitude changed, and he began to seek the society of those to whom he was attracted.

During the filming of *The Eagle*, the beautiful little Hungarian actress, Vilma Banky, played opposite him; and it was observed that her delicate blond beauty, her innate refinement, added to her shy demure admiration of the great artist, began to take effect.

It is significant that so many of those who win recognition on the screen come of humble parentage. Vilma Banky, who was reported to have been a stenographer in Budapest, found herself raised by her great beauty to the position of star, almost over-night.

She was one of Samuel Goldwyn's remarkable finds. This man possesses an almost uncanny ability to select sure-fire box-office successes, as witness his discoveries of Ronald Colman and Lois Moran.

The world has chosen to attribute a love affair

Valentino as I Knew Him

to Rudolph Valentino and Vilma Banky; such, in my opinion, was not the case.

Propinquity is responsible for more marriages than love, and it was propinquity in this case, added possibly to a sincere admiration on Valentino's part for Vilma's budding ability as an actress, as well as for her undeniable beauty.

It might be interesting to describe the bungalow dressing room which was built for Valentino on the United Studio's lot.

This consisted of a dining room and reception room combined, in which were bookcases, an open fireplace, davenport and a combination dining room-library table, with easy chairs, a Brunswick cabinet phonograph and plain one-tone velvet rugs upon the floor. Adjoining this was Rudy's dressing room and bath. His dressing table was equipped with Cooper-Hewitt lights beneath which he could don make-up and get the same effect as he did under the Kleigs. The walls of both rooms were made interesting by groups of armor and firearms, swords and spears. Pictures of friends in the motion picture industry, framed and autographed, were also here in great profusion.

A hall divided these rooms from Valentino's private office, the walls of which were filled with bookcases, containing countless volumes on costumes and history. Next to this was the office

by S. George Ullman

of his secretary, and adjoining that a kitchenette.

During the filming of *The Eagle*, Rudy's time was so limited that he adopted the custom of having his luncheons brought down from his home in containers and served in this bungalow. Here Beltram Masses and Vilma Banky generally joined him. I am persuaded that the atmosphere of good-fellowship and camaraderie which obtained at these intimate informal luncheons did much to foster a natural friendship between the star and his leading woman. And Beltram Masses in the rôle of chaperon!

By this time Auntie had returned from New York. She was living in her own home on Sycamore Street, but not a day passed in which she was not in the house on Whitley Heights. Not in the capacity of housekeeper, for so well was Valentino's house run that there remained nothing for her to do along this line. She was there in the capacity of welcome guest, so that, when Vilma Banky was asked to dine and spend the evening, they were chaperoned by Mrs. Werner.

Rudy and Vilma frequently appeared in society together at parties and openings of plays, so that it is no wonder that a world avid for gossip should link their names. In my opinion it was more a community of interests than a love affair; but possibly in this I am mistaken.

Valentino as I Knew Him

opening of the Valentino picture was a great social success. Lady Curzon made it her personal business to see that as many of her friends as possible were present.

Rudy remained in London as long as he could; but, faced with the necessity to establish his residence in Paris, in order to complete the legal arrangements whereby Natacha could obtain her divorce, Valentino left for France.

Many of Valentino's friends hoped that he would meet Natacha in Paris, and possibly patch the thing up so that there would be no divorce. But here Fate seemed to take a hand, for, without waiting for Rudy's arrival, Natacha had returned to New York.

During his stay in Paris he lived at the Plaza-Atheneé, and it is well known that he appeared much in the company of Jean Nash, the Dolly Sisters and others equally well known to the night life of Paris. It was here also that he met Prince Habile-Lotfallah. This Egyptian prince, a man of great wealth and learning, was enormously taken with Rudy, and urged him to come to Cairo to make a picture. He promised Rudy every cooperation in his power, with the added inducement of the gift of a pure-bred Arabian horse which Rudy was to select from the Prince's stables.

Since nothing would have pleased Valentino

This is the victim of the "powder puff" editorial!

by S. George Ullman

more than to make a desert picture upon the Great Sahara, it is not saying too much to say that, had he lived, Rudy would have arranged to do this.

Rumors now began to sift through into the press concerning the elaborate parties which were staged in Paris for, and by, Valentino. But when I questioned him later (I was rather suspicious of the bounty of some of his friends), I discovered that he had invariably been obliged to pay the bills, his coterie of acquaintances having been most obliging in their willingness to help him spend his money.

I did not blame them so much, however, knowing as I did how easily Rudy could be imposed upon, and how open-handed he always was with his money.

Having now complied with all the requirements of the law in order that Natacha might obtain her divorce, Rudy invited his sister Maria, his brother Alberto Guglielmi, his sister-in-law, and their eleven-year-old-boy to travel with him to London, where he took them about with him generously, showing them the sights of the English capital and opening up to them a world which had existed hitherto only in their imaginations.

While in London, Rudy endeavored to provide his sister Maria with a profession by which she could be self-supporting. He induced her to take

Valentino as I Knew Him

a course in interior decorating, for which course he gladly furnished the money. But, finding the work not to her taste, Maria gave it up, and later returned to Paris to live.

Rudy was very anxious to place his family in professions whereby they could become independent. And, to this end, he arranged later for his brother to go into the office of United Artists in Paris, hoping that there he would learn the business of distribution and might thus become that firm's representative in Italy.

That Christmas which the Guglielmi family spent in London was the first in which brothers and sisters had been united since the death of their parents, and was for this reason one which they never forgot.

To satisfy the curiosity of the public as to any possible resemblance between Alberto, several years older, and Rudolph, let me say that never were two men more unlike, either in physiognomy or character.

Having such a gorgeous time in London, meeting many persons of title, and being entertained at princely homes, Valentino joyously sent me a cable saying he could not possibly leave London until the middle of February. To which I replied saying that, on the contrary, he would be in Hollywood not later than the first of February. Where-

by S. George Ullman

upon Valentino, seeing that his bluff had failed to work, gave in graciously, as usual, and returned on the *Berengeria*, bringing Alberto and his family with him and arriving in Hollywood the last of January.

Mrs. Ullman and I met them in Pasadena, where they left the train in order to avoid publicity. It is most difficult for a star of any magnitude to arrive in Hollywood without assembling crowds who crave to catch a glimpse of their favorite. In spite of the glorious time he had had in Europe, Rudy was childishly glad to be at home again, and assured me, almost in his first breath, not only that everything was paid for, but that he had a balance in the bank. Very cautiously and totally without belief, I questioned him as to the amount of this mysterious reserve fund, whereupon Rudy told me it was thirty thousand—I held my breath until he said the fatal word—francs.

Yet even this was cause for congratulation until bills began to seep in for the thirty-two suits of clothes, the forty pairs of shoes, the scores of neckties, shirts without number, and other purchases which he had neglected to tabulate in his first enthusiasm at returning with money in the bank.

Afterwards it turned out that almost all the money he spent in Europe had been to pay for the glorious time he had there, while he left most of his purchases to be paid for at this end.

Not that it made any material difference, for at this time his affairs were in such a state that he could allow himself any moderate extravagance without harm. I only mention this to show the little-boy attitude of Rudy, one of his most endearing characteristics.

Before leaving for Europe, the purchase of the Beverly Hills house, which Rudy named *Falcon Lair*, had been completed. It clings to the top of the mountainside, overlooking Beverly Hills, the City of Los Angeles, and, on clear days, Catalina Island.

Perched on the surrounding hills, and easily visible from the broad windows of *Falcon Lair*, lie the palatial estates of Harold Lloyd, the late Thomas Ince and Charles Chaplin, *Pickfair*, and just the chimneys of Marion Davies' beautiful English country place.

On the hillside to the left, and equally high, lies the estate of John Gilbert, and, highest of all, on a hilltop back of *Falcon Lair*, rises the gorgeous Spanish home of Fred Thompson and his famous wife, Frances Marion.

Although Rudy had seen many of the medieval castles of England, France and Spain, to say noth-

by S. George Ullman

ing of his beloved Italy, he was thrilled when he returned to his home in Beverly Hills and saw the picturesque beauty of the panorama which spread itself before his eyes. Nowhere in all the world are grouped together such magnificent estates so ideally situated as those owned by the movie colony surrounding *Falcon Lair* in Beverly Hills. The Valentino estate, although comprising eight and one half acres, is situated in the choicest part of Beverly Hills, with a view excelled by none.

While in Europe Rudy had, at various times, made extensive purchases for the home he sometime hoped to have. These were now assembled at *Falcon Lair*, together with the choicest pieces from his apartment in New York, and the house on Whitley Heights. Many of these he caused to be reupholstered in colors he himself selected. He adored rich materials and splendid colors, all shades of dark red being his favorite. Brocades, velvets, and satins which would stand alone, gorgeous embroideries in gold and silver, wrought iron, carvings in ivory and jade, gorgeously bound books with priceless colored plates, china and porcelain worth its weight in gold, Venetian and Bohemian glass, and distinctive bibelots from many lands, all these were included in the furnishings of *Falcon Lair*.

He seemed to care little for the rich Oriental

Valentino as I Knew Him

rugs which adorn many of the homes of his friends, priceless though they were. With the exception of the dining room rug in *Falcon Lair*, which was many-hued, the rugs were of neutral tinted one-toned velvet, which, like the plain walls, formed an artistic background for his many treasures.

From the reception hall to the servants' quarters, I have never been in a house which was so essentially masculine. Luxurious in the extreme and most artistic, it nevertheless reflected the colorful dominant personality of a man accustomed to express himself in his surroundings.

Nevertheless, living in a house, even though it was built by one's self, is certain to bring out the defects of that house, and those of *Falcon Lair* were discernible to Valentino. With characteristic energy, at once he set about eliminating them, and making certain improvements which he felt would add to the comfort, not only of himself, but of those guests with whom he intended to surround himself.

Rudy loved nothing so well as entertaining. Yet, during the stay of his family at *Falcon Lair*, he was limited in this line both by the illness of his sister-in-law and by the torn-up condition of the house.

Possibly these conditions may have contributed to throwing him into the society of Pola Negri

by S. George Ullman

more than otherwise. At any rate, it is certain that these two began to be together on all occasions, Rudy frequently a guest at Pola's handsome colonial home on Beverly Drive, and Pola frequently a guest at *Falcon Lair.*

Chapter 14

EVER since the filming of *The Sheik*, with lovely Agnes Ayres as his leading woman, Rudy's fans had been asking, by the thousands, when he was going to do another Sheik picture, so that when Mrs. Hull wrote *Sons of the Sheik*, it went without saying that the only person who could play the young Sheik was Valentino.

It was therefore purchased for him; the twin brother in the novel eliminated, it went into production under its now famous title, *The Son of the Sheik*.

Nothing could be happier than the circumstances surrounding the making of this picture. For the first time, Rudy felt that the world was with him. He was freed from the unhappy belief, instilled in his mind by Natacha, that every one was trying to get the best of him. His own sunshiny belief in the honor of his friends and associates once again asserted itself.

Conditions were indeed most favorable. He was once again in the rôle made famous by his former great success, which not only established him in a niche all his own but added a word to the

Valentino as I Knew Him

English language, a word so potent that it became noun and verb and adjective.

Again he had for his leading woman one who never failed to portray her part, Vilma Banky, whose youthful blonde beauty was an excellent foil for the dashing, gallant Son of the Sheik.

Notwithstanding the selection of Miss Banky to be his leading woman, the suitability of the story purchased for him, and the coöperation of the entire staff, the outstanding joy in the making of this picture was the fact that Rudy had, for the first time, the services of George Fitzmaurice as director.

It is to be recalled that one of the things contributing to the split between Valentino and Famous Players-Lasky was the fact that Rudy wanted Fitzmaurice to direct *Blood and Sand,* and he really never got over his disappointment in not having him. He was like a child. Disappoint him and he would remember it for years. Now, when a fortuitous circumstance gave him Fitzmaurice as director, he was supremely happy.

There is no gainsaying the fact that Fitzmaurice had a marvelous understanding of Valentino. An artist to his fingertips, Fitzmaurice understood the volatile Italian, knew how to handle him, to get the best out of him, to thrill him with an enthusiasm which brought Rudy to his toes, and how to

Valentino as I Knew Him

develop to its highest point the peculiar genius of Valentino as an actor.

Both spoke French and, when the limits of the English language were reached, they dropped into French to indicate to each other those delicate *nuances* which are often elusive to the English tongue.

I remember the long discussions which would take place between these two over a trifle which some would have ignored, or possibly never would have seen. But, to Fitzmaurice and Valentino, they were important, as indicating the fine line between a mere performance and an artistic interpretation. They worked together so harmoniously that all finally agreed with Rudy in his contention that Fitzmaurice was indeed the outstanding director for him.

I think that Rudy had a better time during the filming of *The Son of the Shiek* than in any other of his pictures. He used to have his lunches brought down from home, and there gathered in the dining room of his suite at the studio Constance Talmadge, Ronald Colman, Vilma Banky, George Fitzmaurice, Pola Negri, Allistair MacIntosh, Louella Parsons, Marion Davies, Lady Loughborough, Eugene Brewster, Corliss Palmer, and many others. All these I met at different

by S. George Ullman

times at Rudy's famous luncheons. Brilliant conversation was the order of the day.

The costumes worn in *The Son of the Sheik* Rudy had bought abroad. Most of them originals and absolutely authentic. Some people would consider a fortune the amount of money he had tied up in costumes and props, for nothing less than the best suited his fastidious taste.

As I have said before, when Valentino was filming a picture he enacted his rôle at all times. Once, when we were on the train going to New York, he read *The Sea Hawk*, which afterwards Frank Lloyd produced with Milton Sills in the leading rôle. Rudy went wild about this part, and declared that it was made for him. Under its spell he was indeed *The Sea Hawk*. His manners were rough. When he wanted me to move aside, he shoved me out of his way with his elbow. He ate like a pig. Considering Valentino's fastidious table manners, this ability to get inside the skin of a character greatly interested me.

Valentino begged J. D. Williams to buy this picture for him, as at that time Rudy was under contract to Ritz-Carlton Pictures. It was only when Williams lacked the foresight to accede to Valentino's request that Rudy gave over being the *Sea Hawk*, and again began to use a fork.

Again, when he was filming *The Sainted Devil*,

Valentino as I Knew Him

his habitual courtesy left him entirely, and he was rough and swaggering. I shudder to think what would have happened if he had ever been called upon to play a cut-throat Apache. His friends would have had to run for their lives!

Another ambition of Valentino's was to play *Ben Hur*, and I imagine that there are few who would not agree with me that Rudolph Valentino would have made the greatest *Ben Hur* the world had ever seen. Picture Valentino as the galley slave in the chariot race and then as the idealist forever dreaming of raising his race to its proper place in the history of the world. As the lover of Miriam, he would have made a love story so spiritual, so tender and so appealing that it would have been an idyl to be forgotten never.

One day during the filming of *The Son of the Sheik*, he came into my office, garbed in the striped robe which he wears in the first part of the picture and, seating himself on the corner of my desk, he said, in a calmly dispassionate tone:

"Ullman, I can't forever go on playing such parts as these. On your honor now, how long do you give me to play the romantic lover?"

I looked at him in astonishment, wondering if he were in earnest.

He nodded his head at me.

"I'm serious. I really want to know."

by S. George Ullman

After thinking a moment, I said:

"Well, I should say about five years."

Rudy smiled one of his rare smiles and said:

"That is about what I think. And long enough, too! After that I want to do great characters like Cesare Borgia, Christopher Columbus; men who have accomplished great things. Then, of course, there is the American Indian. I would very much like to play a young Chief; and, before I finish, I want most of all to play a Gypsy and an Apache."

Alas! that he did not live to carry out these dreams! Every reader can visualize what he would have made of these rôles.

In a limited way his portrayal of the father, the old Sheik in *The Son of the Sheik*, gives us an idea of how well Valentino would have handled these character parts. It gave him no end of pleasure when, with his marvelous make-up for the old Sheik on, he walked around on the lot and not one of his associates recognized him.

Concerning the character of The Sheik, which, as all the world knows, Valentino created, he had peculiar ideas. He loathed utterly the application of the word Sheik to himself, except as to his portrayal of the part in his two pictures. To call him a Sheik in real life offended him to the soul; he deplored the lowering of the majestic title of an

Valentino as I Knew Him

Arab chieftain to describe the common street flirtations of the morons to whom it became generally applied.

He endeavored to give a dignified portrayal of the character in both the pictures in which he played the young Sheik. And I believe I am right in saying that, if viewed intelligently and without bias, Valentino gave to both characters a dignity proper to the original. To be sure, he idealized the part, a thing which Valentino could not fail to do with any rôle which he essayed. Personally, I recall the Arabic salutation of respect which he pays to his father as a gesture of as great a dignity as I have ever seen.

There is no disguising the fact that Valentino actually loved the desert. The long stretches of sand dunes which appear in the first part of *The Son of the Sheik* were filmed near Yuma, Arizona, and there Rudy exhibited such joy in the desert scenes that others in the cast came to share his enthusiasm. His favorite music, played during the filming of this part of the picture, was Homer Grunn's *Desert Suite*.

Later, scenes were filmed near Guadalupe, California, and still others on the set at the Pickford-Fairbanks Studios, where tons and carloads of sand were dumped to simulate the desert. But the sand storm during which Valentino sets out to find

by S. George Ullman

Yasmin was filmed near Yuma, the storm being precipitated by wind machines.

No actual sand storm on the Sahara could have been more violent and blinding in velocity than the one stirred by those terrific wind demons which drove the particles of sand against the faces and bodies of the actors in a way to cause actual suffering.

The women, Vilma Banky, and Agnes Ayres, disliked these sand storms, but Rudolph actually enjoyed them. They seemed to exhilarate him so that I used to wonder if at any time in his previous career he had been a son of the desert.

It is only another instance of the way in which Valentino's personality could perform wonders, that Agnes Ayres was induced to return to the screen for the short scenes in which she portrayed the mother of the young Sheik. It was considered among the impossibilities to secure her services, and others were under consideration for the rôle when Rudy performed the miracle.

Lest the public underestimate the quality of her sacrifice, let it be remembered that it required great courage for a young and beautiful woman deliberately to don make-up which would cause her to appear matronly, despite the fact that for many years to come she will be able to play youthful leads. However, she did this gladly for

Valentino as I Knew Him

Valentino, so that the beauty of the picture was enhanced by the actual appearance of the same character which graced the earlier romance.

Another great concession was that of W. K. Kellogg of Battle Creek, Michigan, and Pomona, California, owner and breeder of the finest Arabian horses on this continent. The beautiful white Arabian stallion, Jadan, used in filming *The Sheik*, was necessary in that sequence in *The Son of the Sheik*, wherein the father rides to his son's rescue. Of course, another horse could have been substituted; but, with Valentino's passion for accuracy, he greatly desired Jadan, and Mr. Kellogg, appreciating this, allowed the horse to be used.

I shall never forget Rudy's joy when he discovered that he could have Jadan. It was one of those small things, unimportant to some, which delights the soul of the artist.

Work on this picture was so arduous that Valentino took more time off than was his custom. He was much seen in the company of Pola Negri, with whom he took long horseback rides Sunday mornings, and whom he escorted to various premières.

At the Charlot Revue, which fairly swept Los Angeles off its feet by its brilliance and cleverness, Rudy gave a large party which included Pola Negri and other screen celebrities.

"Falcon Lair," the Hollywood home of Valentino, after its erection

by S. George Ullman

Rudy and Pola were seen often at the dances of the Sixty Club, which were always given at the Biltmore Hotel; on one occasion these two won the first prize in a costume dance at which Pola appeared as a Spanish dancer and Rudy as a toreador, in the costume which he wore in *Blood and Sand*.

It was a joyous day when the picture was finished. Rudy supervised the cutting, which was so competently done by Hal Kern that few suggestions were necessary.

Notwithstanding this supervision, Rudy attended the preview at Santa Monica, where we sat together and, for the first time with an audience, watched the scenes of his last masterpiece unroll before our eyes. It was then that we realized, from the enthusiasm displayed, the great appeal which this picture would have upon the public at large.

To me it seemed well nigh perfect. I could pick no flaws in it. But at least a dozen times Rudy nudged me with his elbow and whispered:

"If I could only do that bit over, I could do better."

This ceaseless ambition to improve his work, this gnawing dissatisfaction even with his best efforts, were to my mind indications that Valentino belonged to that great company of artists who possess genius of a high order, for it is only the mediocre who boast and brag of their prowess.

It touches me deeply to recall how, in the last few weeks of his life, Rudy bridged the discord which had separated him from many of his old friends. It was as if he gathered up the raveled ends of friendships he had cherished, and knit them together into a more enduring fabric.

On the occasion of this preview he saw Cora Macy, famous character actress of stage and screen, and her equally well-known daughter Cora McGeachy, whose genius in costuming is almost too well known to need comment. For the most important revues on the New York stage, for Hollywood studios where she designed the gorgeous costumes for Colleen Moore's production of *Irene* and other First National pictures, Cora McGeachy's work is in constant demand. Rudy had formerly been friendly with these two distinguished women but, during his married life, he had not seen much of them. The same was true of June Mathis, to whom he was more indebted than to any other one person in the world. On account of the quarrel between Natacha Rambova and June Mathis, Valentino had become somewhat estranged from her, also.

When he saw these three old friends coming out of the theater after the preview, he stopped

by S. George Ullman

them, and then and there showed by his cordiality that the old Rudy was again in evidence and at heart had never changed.

Cora McGeachy was in tears, seeing which Rudy inquired what the matter was.

"Oh, I am so happy," she sobbed, "at seeing you back in your old place on the screen."

Rudy was very much touched by this evidence of friendship and sincere interest in his career.

I have often thought since his death of what satisfaction it must have given his old friends to realize that before he went away he gave them so much evidence of his affection.

I know that Rudy had no premonition of his approaching death. Yet as I look back I can see that the last few weeks of his life were almost entirely given over to the smoothing out of old misunderstandings. Notable among them were those with Jean Acker and Natacha Rambova.

After unannounced previews at Santa Monica and Burbank, *The Son of the Sheik* had a special preview showing at Grauman's Million Dollar Theater in Los Angeles.

The opening night was a veritable triumph. All day long crowds had attended the continuous showing and, at the evening performance, every notable of the screen was present, pausing under

Valentino as I Knew Him

the Kleigs to be photographed, as is the custom at premières.

In the richly decorated foyer of the theater stood the most imposing floral piece I had ever seen. It was about eight feet high and ten feet wide, the background composed of red gladioli diagonally across which was written, in white carnations, Valentino's name.

When this huge structure met his eyes Rudy halted, almost overcome by the tribute. When I whispered in his ear that this was from Pola, a slow smile crept over his face.

The manager of the theater had previously informed me that he hoped Mr. Valentino would be willing to rise in his place in the audience when his name was called and take a bow. When I told Rudy this he said:

"Very well. But no speeches."

Man proposes, but God disposes.

As usual there were two evening showings, one at seven, and one at nine. Valentino had as his guests a party of twelve, among whom were Pola Negri, Prince Divani and his wife Mae Murray, Louella Parsons, Charles Chaplin, others equally noted. With these friends Rudy was chatting pleasantly, when, to his surprise, instead of being asked to rise in his place in the audience, he was

by S. George Ullman

called to the stage by the manager just before the prologue of the second showing. As he made his appearance, such a tumult of applause broke forth that Rudy was confused. When the manager spoke up, saying that so long as Valentino was before his audience, doubtless he would not object to saying a few words, Rudy saw that he was caught.

Game as usual, he made a short impromptu speech which was a masterpiece of cryptic utterance.

Had Valentino ever attempted public speaking for such worthy objects as a Community Chest or a Liberty Loan, for anything in which his emotions were engaged, I venture to say that few could have equaled him in the ability to move audiences. On this occasion, when he faced a Million Dollar Theater audience filled to capacity with his fans, little did he or any one of them imagine that this was his last appearance in public on the Pacific Coast, and that never again would any of them face him in life. But so it was, for soon after this it was decided that it would be wise for him to make personal appearances in certain of the larger cities where *The Son of the Sheik* was to be shown, and Rudy, filled with his periodical wanderlust and desirous also of seeing his

Valentino as I Knew Him

brother and his family safely on board the ship which was to take them home, willingly agreed to make the arduous trip East, although this proved to be in the midst of such grueling heat that I doubt he would have attempted it had he known what was before him.

However, the future is mercifully hidden from us all.

We thereupon set out upon what was to be his last journey in this life.

He left for San Francisco, while a few days later his brother Alberto and family went by the southerly route to New York, where we expected to meet them.

A large group of people came to the station to see Rudy off, among whom was Pola Negri, who again violated the superstition of the danger of watching a beloved one out of sight.

She stood on the platform watching Rudy, who hung out the door of the observation car, disregarding the efforts of the trainman to close the door, and waving his hand until a curve in the track whisked him out of sight. This also was the last time Pola Negri saw Rudolph Valentino in life.

We arrived in San Francisco on Thursday, July 15, being met by Mayor Rolph and a host of notables and newspaper men and cameramen.

by S. George Ullman

A luncheon had been arranged at the Fairmont Hotel, at which Mayor Rolph presided. This lasted until four o'clock in the afternoon, when the Mayor took us out to his home, where we met Mrs. Rolph, a gracious and charming woman.

We were shown about the spacious grounds, and when we reached the kennels Rudy's delight burst all bounds. An ardent lover of animals, particularly horses and dogs, he expressed so much appreciation of the Mayor's finely bred animals that Mr. Rolph made him a present of the beautiful black spaniel to which I have alluded previously.

Both Mr. and Mrs. Rolph were extremely fond of Valentino and received him almost as a beloved son. He was lonely at all times for the family love which he continuously seemed to miss and long for. The homelike atmosphere of the Rolphs, and the sincere affection they expressed, fell like balm upon Rudy's soul.

The next morning we left for the East, in the midst of such terrific heat that, as soon as we boarded the train, Rudy donned a Chinese lounging suit and, after a weak attempt to read a book which only lasted about ten minutes, turned over and calmly went to sleep.

The trip was uneventful until we reached Chicago, where we found the heat to be sufficiently

Valentino as I Knew Him

eventful to rouse even the dullest to take notice of it.

Although we were in Chicago only between trains, we went to the Blackstone. Here I was handed the now famous editorial which originally appeared in *The Chicago Tribune.* Since this scurrilous attack embittered the last days of Rudolph Valentino, killing his usual joy in living and causing him more mental anguish than any other article ever written about him, I quote in full the infamous anonymous attack, which I recognized as coming from the same poison pen which earlier in the year had, without cause and without reason, attacked my friend.

PINK POWDER PUFFS

A new public ballroom was opened on the north side a few days ago, a truly handsome place and apparently well run. The pleasant impression lasts until one steps into the men's washroom and finds there on the wall a contraption of glass tubes and levers and a slot for the insertion of a coin. The glass tubes contain a fluffy pink solid, and beneath them one reads an amazing legend which runs something like this: "Insert coin. Hold personal puff beneath the tube. Then pull the lever."

by S. George Ullman

A powder vending machine! In a men's washroom! Homo Americanus! Why didn't some one quietly drown Rudolph Guglielmo, alias Valentino, years ago?

And was the pink powder machine pulled from the wall or ignored? It was not. It was used. We personally saw two "men"—as young lady contributors to the Voice of the People are wont to describe the breed—step up, insert coin, hold kerchief beneath the spout, pull the lever, then take the pretty pink stuff and put it on their cheeks in front of the mirror.

Another member of this department, one of the most benevolent men on earth, burst raging into the office the other day because he had seen a young "man" combing his pomaded hair in the elevator. But we claim our pink powder story beats all this hollow.

It is time for a matriarchy if the male of the species allows such things to persist Better a rule by masculine women than by effeminate men. Man began to slip, we are beginning to believe, when he discarded the straight razor for the safety pattern. We shall not be surprised when we hear that the safety razor has given way to the depilatory.

Who or what is to blame is what puzzles us. Is this degeneration into effeminacy a cognate re-

action with pacificism to the virilities and realities of the war? Are pink powder and parlor pinks in any way related? How does one reconcile masculine cosmetics, sheiks, floppy pants, and slave bracelets with a disregard for law and an aptitude for crime more in keeping with the frontier of half a century ago than a twentieth-century metropolis?

Do women like the type of "man" who pats pink powder on his face in a public washroom and arranges his coiffure in a public elevator? Do women at heart belong to the Wilsonian era of "I Didn't Raise My Boy to Be a Soldier"? What has become of the old "caveman" line?

It is a strange social phenomenon and one that is running its course not only here in America but in Europe as well. Chicago may have its powder puffs; London has its dancing men and Paris its gigolos. Down with Decatur; up with Elinor Glyn. Hollywood is the national school of masculinity. Rudy, the beautiful gardener's boy, is the prototype of the American male.

Hell's bells. Oh, sugar.

As I read this cowardly and yellow attack my countenance must have changed, for Rudy, watching me, immediately asked what was wrong.

If he had not caught me in the act of reading

by S. George Ullman

it, I think that I never would have allowed him to see it, so profoundly do I regret the irritating and saddening effect it had upon him. He took the screed from my reluctant fingers, read it; instantly I realized how deeply he was moved. His face paled, his eyes blazed and his muscles stiffened.

I shared his anger, for it seemed to me then, and I have never changed my opinion, that not in all my experience with anonymous attacks in print had I ever read one in which the name of an honest gentleman had been dragged in the mud in so causeless a manner.

What, I ask you, had the installation of a powdering machine in any public ballroom in Chicago to do with a dignified actor in New York and Hollywood? Had Valentino made dancing his profession, I grant you that there might have been some reason for this envious attack. But I have related in this volume how sincerely Valentino disliked the profession of dancing and what grave sacrifices he made both financially and otherwise in repudiating the career of a dancer and suffering the privations necessary to become an actor in motion pictures.

In running over in my own mind the characters he portrayed on the screen in recent years, I men-

Valentino as I Knew Him

tion *Monsieur Beaucaire, Cobra, The Sainted Devil, The Four Horsemen, The Sheik* and *The Son of the Sheik*. And I ask the public to tell me if in any of these super-pictures Valentino assumed a character which would connect him in any way with the sort of effeminate man who would resort to a pink powder puff.

For myself, I answer emphatically that there is no connection whatsoever; and I agreed with my friend that no one, unless he were animated by personal jealousy of the exalted position Valentino enjoyed in the estimation of the American public, could have written so impudent an attack upon a gentleman. I purposely make use of the term impudent, because an inferior can be impudent only to his superior.

Wounded to the soul by the implication that his ancestry had been common, whereas the world knows that marriage between the daughter of a surgeon and an Italian cavalry officer constitute honorable parentage for offspring, to say the least, Valentino prepared at once to avenge the insult offered.

Summoning the representative of *The Tribune's* powerful and greatly feared rival, *The Chicago Herald-Examiner*, Valentino handed to him for publication the following:

by S. George Ullman

July 19th, 1926.

TO THE MAN (?) WHO WROTE THE EDITORIAL HEADED "PINK POWDER PUFFS" IN SUNDAY'S "TRIBUNE":

The above mentioned editorial is at least the second scurrilous personal attack you have made upon me, my race, and my father's name.

You slur my Italian ancestry; you cast ridicule upon my Italian name; you cast doubt upon my manhood.

I call you, in return, a contemptible coward and to prove which of us is a better man, I challenge you to a personal test. This is not a challenge to a duel in the generally accepted sense—that would be illegal. But in Illinois boxing is legal, so is wrestling. I, therefore, defy you to meet me in the boxing or wrestling arena to prove, in typically American fashion (for I am an American citizen), which of us is more a man. I prefer this test of honor to be private, so I may give you the beating you deserve, and because I want to make it absolutely plain that this challenge is not for purposes of publicity. I am handing copies of this to the newspapers simply because I doubt that any one so cowardly as to write about me as you have would respond to a defy unless forced by the press to do so. I do not know who you are or how big you are

Valentino as I Knew Him

but this challenge stands if you are as big as Jack Dempsey.

I will meet you immediately or give you a reasonable time in which to prepare, for I assume that your muscles must be flabby and weak, judging by your cowardly mentality and that you will have to replace the vitriol in your veins for red blood—if there be a place in such a body as yours for red blood and manly muscle.

I want to make it plain that I hold no grievance against the Chicago Tribune, *although it seems a mistake to let a cowardly writer use its valuable columns as this "man" does. My fight is personal —with the poison-pen writer of editorials that stoop to racial and personal prejudice. The* Tribune *through Miss Mae Tinee, has treated me and my work kindly and at times very favorably. I welcome criticism of my work as an actor—but I will resent with every muscle of my body attacks upon my manhood and ancestry.*

Hoping I will have an opportunity to demonstrate to you that the wrist under a slave bracelet may snap a real fist into your sagging jaw and that I may teach you respect of a man even though he happens to prefer to keep his face clean, I remain with

Utter Contempt
RUDOLPH VALENTINO.

by S. George Ullman

P. S. I will return to Chicago within ten days. You may send your answer to me in New York, care of United Artists Corp., 729 7th Ave.

The publication of this challenge, which was originally in *The Herald-Examiner*, was flashed immediately over wires and cables to the four corners of the earth, and the furious discussion which resulted is of too recent date to need comment.

While we were on the train going from Chicago to New York I asked Rudy, as soon as he had had time to cool down and think coherently, for this attack had thrown him into a rage so abysmal that his whole being was disorganized:

"What are you going to do if you find that this editor is seven feet tall and twice your weight?"

To which he replied:

"What would be the difference? If I am licked by a more powerful man that will be no disgrace and at any rate I'll show him that I am no pink powder puff."

That unhappy epithet, pink powder puff, stuck in Rudy's craw. During the few short weeks between the time it was applied to him by this antagonist who was too cowardly to make himself known, and Valentino's untimely death, Rudy repeated the words more times than I heard him

Valentino as I Knew Him

utter any other phrase in all the years that I knew him.

He would repeat them seemingly in agony of soul, as if fearful that, in the minds of some who did not know him, the thought of effeminacy might stick. Whereas I, as his friend, make the statement that no cowboy on the Western plains nor athlete from the Marines could boast a more powerful physique than that of Valentino, nor more truly possess the right to the title of he-man.

What if he did wear a slave bracelet? It was given to him by his wife, whom he still adored, and no more power on earth could have persuaded him to remove it. Would God there were more men as faithful!

When we arrived in New York we were met by the usual crowd of fans, reporters and cameramen, who followed Rudy to the Ambassador Hotel as if he were a visiting potentate.

Rudy was so naïve that he got a great kick out of the acclaim which followed him after he became famous. The sight of motorcycle traffic officers clearing the way for his triumphal car always thrilled him.

Arriving at the Ambassador, he good-naturedly posed again for the many stills which have now become so valuable.

Rudy and he cocker span e g

by S. George Ullman

The press at this time was much exercised as to Valentino's reputed strength, and many were the conjectures as to what would happen when we went back to Chicago should the unknown dare to emerge from his editorial incognito and face Rudy in a fistic encounter.

So much was said on this subject that I was not at all surprised one day to receive a call from Mr. Frank O'Neil, known in sporting circles as "Buck" O'Neil, who is the boxing expert on *The New York Evening Journal*. Buck told me that, privately, he very much doubted Valentino's reputed ability as an athlete; and that, just for his own satisfaction, he would like to stage a little friendly bout.

He assured me very confidentially that he would not hurt Rudy, whereupon I rather bumptiously told him that he would do much better to look out for himself, as Rudy packed a wicked punch. Let me state here that Buck O'Neil in his gym clothes weighed approximately one hundred and ninety-five pounds and was six feet one inch in height, while Rudy at that time weighed one hundred and sixty-seven pounds and was five feet eleven in height.

So confident was I of the outcome that, without consulting Rudy, I gave my consent to this plan, and we arranged to have the bout on the roof of the Ambassador Hotel the following afternoon.

When I told Rudy of this plan his only comment was:

"That's great!"

Not one word had been said about the difference in size and weight and not one question had Rudy asked about his antagonist. Just a single "That's great!"; this was that lad's spirit.

Accordingly, at the appointed hour, they met on the roof of the Ambassador; both posed obligingly for the usual stills. Then, to the accompaniment of the grinding of motion picture cameras, the two pugilists fell to.

At first they boxed very lightly, until Buck curled a beautiful left to Rudy's chin, his first intimation that the thing was serious.

With that, Rudy pulled himself together and began to fight. He aimed a short jab at Buck's jaw, but O'Neil ducked and caught it on the side of his head and went down to the gravel of the roof. Instantly Rudy was beside him, helping him up and apologizing profusely for letting that one slip.

Buck was game. He just laughed it off and said that that was what he had tried to do to Rudy, but failed.

by S. George Ullman

They went at it again for a while, and Buck's tactics were confined to what is known as turtle shell covering; he was protecting himself and occasionally lashing out with either hand.

I recall at one time that he landed on Rudy's nose, and I can truthfully say that the blow hurt me more than it did him, fearing as I did that some damage might be done to that important screen asset.

Later, when Buck O'Neil was taking a shower in my bathroom, he turned to me and said:

"Don't make any mistake! That boy has a punch like a mule's kick. I'd sure hate to have him sore at me!"

When we went down to dinner that night, O'Neil was enthusiastically urging upon Valentino the possibilities of a pugilistic career, should he ever care to give up pictures.

The next day Rudy saw his brother and family off to Paris on the *S.S. France.*

Not waiting to see the ship sail, we jumped into a taxi and drove post haste to another pier, where General Nobile was sailing on an Italian liner. Rudy said good-by to him and congratulated him again on his successful flight over the North Pole.

The next day his picture, *The Son of the Sheik*, was to open at the Mark Strand Theater.

From early morning the crowds had begun to

Valentino as I Knew Him

gather for the eleven o'clock performance. The double lines stretched two blocks in each direction, and, when we arrived with a small party about two o'clock, to attend the afternoon performance, traffic was blocked.

The heat was terrific, the thermometer registering around ninety-eight degrees; yet that huge aggregation of people was standing quietly, neither pushing nor crowding, waiting patiently their turn to be admitted. They fanned themselves and wiped perspiring faces. I distinctly remember that there was no laughing nor apparent lightness of thought. It seemed rather that earnestness and respect animated the crowd, as if a desire to see a great artist rather than a popular movie star motivated them.

Inside the theater there was hardly standing room. The picture was received with acclaim and, at the close, Rudy made his appearance and gave one of his gracious charming speeches, extemporaneous as usual, and captivated his hearers.

To quote one of these little speeches of Valentino in cold print probably would not convey to the reader anything of its charm which came mostly from Rudy's gallant presence, his flashing eyes, and his all too rare smiles. I myself, well as I knew him, invariably yielded to his fascination as a speaker and felt myself carried along as in-

by S. George Ullman

evitably as he swayed his unknown friends in his great audiences.

I do not say that the enthusiasm of his fans was not sufficient in itself to create the scenes which followed, but I think that his little speeches increased their ardor considerably.

When we reached the stage door on our way out, such a sight met our eyes that we were in despair. Between three and four thousand people were jammed around the entrance, against whose volume the ten policemen detailed to clear a pathway for us were of no avail. They simply added ten more to the number.

Milling and pushing, the crowd choked every foot of space up to the door itself. Our automobile was only a little black spot, like an oasis in a desert. We sent ahead of us the other members of our little party, Aileen Pringle, Jimmie Quirk and Major McCutcheon, who reached the car in safety.

The people were waiting for *Valentino*.

Then I started, with Rudy behind me, his hands on my shoulders. In this fashion we plowed our way through the crowd, as if we were carrying a football to the goal.

I was safe, but the crowds snatched at Rudy, tearing off his tie, grabbing his pocket handkerchief, ripping buttons from his coat and even tear-

Valentino as I Knew Him

ing the cuff links from his shirt. Somebody, somewhere, has a hat belonging to Rudolph Valentino.

The poor boy was almost torn to bits, but he was laughing at his predicament until a woman fan, more frenzied than the others, jumped on the running board of our car just as it started to move and was torn off by the crowd. She fell to the pavement with a thud which startled all of us, but Rudy was the most concerned. He endeavored to have the chauffeur stop the car, but before it could be done the woman had been swallowed up in the crowd and could not be found.

Valentino's anxiety, however, was not sufficiently allayed; upon our arrival at the hotel, he had me telephone to all police stations to see if a woman victim of an automobile accident had been reported. Upon receiving a negative answer, he was greatly relieved.

Strange to say, Rudy seemed rather quiet after his ovation at the Mark Strand, whereas the rest of us were very much excited.

We separated soon after this. Aileen Pringle, Jimmie Quirk and Major McCutcheon went to their homes to dress, with the agreement to meet later for dinner.

Rudy's quiet mood continued, so much so that we fell into a most serious conversation. In moments like these I most appreciated the quality of

by S. George Ullman

the boy's friendship for me. He trusted me as a son might trust a beloved father, and he confided to me his reactions to every occurrence in his life, both physical and mental, insofar as a gentleman might.

At this particular time he talked to me of his ambitions. One thing in particular, I remember, was his plan, immediately upon his return to Hollywood, to go in seriously for piano lessons, for which instrument he had a natural aptitude. He said that he intended to let no one, not even his closest friends, know of this work until he was prepared to be able to play commendably, regardless of the amount of time this would take.

In this I realized two things. One was his love of the dramatic, and the other his boyish desire to spring a surprise on his friends.

He talked to me of marriage. He asked me if I thought it would ever be wise for him to marry a girl who was not in pictures. My answer is irrelevant. I only quote his words to show that his mind was not made up even at this late hour, and that questionings as to the propriety of marrying this or that woman who had taken his fancy for the moment were bubbling in the back of his mind.

Just here it might be well to answer, once and for all, the question which was hurled at me by reporters and feature writers every time the train stopped on our transcontinental journeys or upon our arrival at theater or hotels. And that was: were Pola Negri and Valentino engaged?

I repeat that, although I was entirely in his confidence, he never told me so, and I never asked him.

When reporters put the question directly to Rudy, his gallant reply was, invariably:

"Ask the lady!"

He did tell me, however, that until he had completed his career he had no intention of marrying anybody.

After this we dressed for the evening, and Rudy gave his disheveled suit to Frank, his valet, for much needed repairs.

We started out, first picking up Jean Acker at her home and later meeting the rest of the party, which had then been augmented by Donald Freeman, Hal Fyfe and Ben Ali Haggin.

We had dinner together and then went to Texas Guinan's, where an incident occurred which I thought rather remarkable.

Texas, who, by the way, is an attractive woman and a marvelous hostess, brought over to our table the fakir Rahmin Bey, then at the height of his fame as an exponent of magic.

by S. George Ullman

Rudy, as usual, was much interested; again his overpowering curiosity to get at the secrets of a puzzle animated him. Rahmin Bey told Valentino that, if he would permit, he, Rahmin, would thrust a needle through Valentino's cheek without pain and without drawing blood.

Rudy was game and would have allowed this had I not intervened, whereupon Rudy offered to allow the test to be made upon his arm.

Rahmin Bey being agreeable, Rudy then stood up, stripped off his coat and rolled up his shirt sleeve.

With the eyes of every one in the night club upon him, Rudy submitted to the thrusting of a long needle through the flesh of his forearm, and gazed upon it with amazement. The needle being withdrawn, without blood and without pain, as Rahmin had promised, Rudy laughed, pulled down his shirt sleeve and resumed his supper as if nothing had happened. But I, fearing an infection, sent for alcohol and thoroughly cleansed his arm with the antiseptic.

During the time we were in New York, Rudy revived the acquaintance of Mal St. Clair, Sigrid Holmquist, Greta Nissen, Ann Pennington, Barclay Warburton and his sister Mary Brown Warburton, Schuyler Parsons, and many others of social and theatrical renown.

Valentino as I Knew Him

He spent several very happy week-ends with Mr. Parsons on his estate at Great Neck.

I was cognizant of his affection for Jean Acker and the quiet happiness he had in her company. The frankness with which he told her of his troubles and his life since they had parted gave further evidence of the understanding which still existed between them.

The following week we left for Chicago, for an appearance at the Roosevelt Theater, where his picture was to be shown. Here we were literally besieged by sporting editors, feature writers and reporters, who camped on our trail wanting to know if there was to be a fight with the *Tribune* editor, until Rudy consented to go to a gymnasium to demonstrate his prowess.

Although he was always willing to wrestle or box, at this time he was particularly glad to give publicity to anything which would throw a true light on his ability to hold his own in everything pertaining to manly sports, thus offsetting his undesirable and undeserved reputation as dandy, as exploited in the abusive "pink powder puff" editorial.

Having given for two weeks or more, the opportunity to the anonymous writer of the before quoted "pink powder puff" insult, Valentino then

by S. George Ullman

issued the following statement, which he gave to the press, the only paper in Chicago which failed to quote it being *The Tribune*, a thing, of course, which it could not very well afford to do, since it had been the source of the attack.

It is evident you cannot make a coward fight any more than you can draw blood out of a turnip. The heroic silence of the writer who chose to attack me without any provocation in the Chicago Tribune *leaves no doubt as to the total absence of manliness in his whole makeup.*

I feel I have been vindicated because I consider his silence as a tacit retraction, and an admission which I am forced to accept even though it is not entirely to my liking.

The newspaper men and women whom it has been my privilege to know briefly or for a longer time have been so absolutely fair and so loyal to their profession and their publications, that I need hardly say how conspicuous is this exception to the newspaper profession.

I want it understood that the vehemence with which I denounce the anonymous writer of this cowardly attack upon my friend is not based so much upon what the article contained as upon the deep hurt it gave Rudy, embittering as it did the

Valentino as I Knew Him

last days of his life and, in my opinion, hastening his death.

Who knows but that, in those last days when he was conscious, able to think, and undisturbed by visitors, his mind might have dwelt on his inability to avenge the insult and that, had his last hours been more free from anxiety, his power to cope with the inroads of the septic poisoning might have been increased, and possibly his life spared.

This will always be a moot question with me. And with others who have not been slow to express a similar opinion. For this reason, to the day of my death, this question will be unanswered.

It is only fair to say that the last paragraph in Valentino's statement, quoted above, is absolutely true. The United Artists as well as Mr. Valentino himself subscribed to press clipping bureaus, by means of which we were informed of practically everything printed about our stars. And I reiterate that never before has anything come to our attention so bitterly worded, so personal, so far-fetched and entirely uncalled for as *The Chicago Tribune's* editorial.

After the opening performance of *The Son of the Sheik*, the huge Roosevelt Theater was packed to suffocation with an audience composed of the literary, dramatic, social and artistic lights of the city. It was said that never before, even at Grand

by S. George Ullman

Opera, had such a characteristically cosmopolitan audience been gathered.

The suburbs had emptied themselves, and the hotels were filled with out of town guests who had come on to Chicago for this notable occasion. When Valentino made his appearance upon the stage, he was greeted with applause the like of which only Theodore Roosevelt, for whom the theater was named, had known.

The acclaim lasted several minutes, forcing Valentino to stand, smiling and embarrassed, while the enthusiasm spent itself.

Doubtless inspired by his sensational reception, Rudy made what I consider the best speech of his life, receiving upon its conclusion a similarly vociferous acclaim, together with shouts of his name.

That evening after the theater, we were the supper guests of the brilliant young State's attorney, Michael Romano, who was a close personal friend of Valentino.

The next day we left on the Twentieth Century Limited for New York, where we found that the Associated Press dispatches had given wide publicity to Valentino's second defiance of his unknown assailant.

Here we stayed a week, which time Rudy employed in enjoying himself, turning day into night

Valentino as I Knew Him

and having, as he expressed it, the time of his life.

An amusing incident which occurred during this period comes to my mind. One morning, very early, I was awakened by Rudy, who came to my room. He touched me on the shoulder. There I saw him standing, still in his evening clothes, with a glass of ice cold Vichy in his hand.

"Would you like some water?" he asked.

I rubbed my eyes.

"Why this C. P. R. service?" I inquired.

"Oh, I thought you might be thirsty!"

"You mean," I said, "that you are bringing me this peace offering, hoping that I will not scold you for getting home at five o'clock in the morning!"

"Well," said Rudy sheepishly, "I did intend to ask you to see that I was not disturbed until noon. I'm going to lunch with Jean at one."

The glass of ice cold Vichy I found refreshing after all, as New York is no summer resort; so I let Rudy laugh that one off.

When we went down to Atlantic City we motored, leaving New York at noon and arriving at five o'clock. We were halted on the outskirts by an escort consisting of the Acting Mayor, ten motorcycle policemen, and hundreds of fans in automobiles, which fell in behind our car, and made quite a triumphal procession.

by S. George Ullman

Valentino's appearance had been well advertised. An enormous crowd greeted him at the Ritz-Carlton. Here he found his old friend Gus Edwards, who was then running one of his famous revues at the hotel, and who begged Rudy to come down as his guest, as soon as he had finished making his appearance at the Virginia Theater, where the picture was to open.

In spite of the heat, Rudy promised.

Our attempt to get from the Ritz-Carlton to the Virginia was the most riotous thing I ever experienced. The crowds were suffocating, the largest and most insistent we had ever seen. The ten policemen who attempted to clear a path so that we could get to the waiting car were of no avail whatsoever. They were simply in the way.

When finally we plowed our way to the automobile and got in, both of us had to settle our disordered clothing. The car crawled at a snail's pace, being blocked before and at each side by the crowds of men and women who leaped upon the running boards and thrust their hands in at the open windows. Rudy shook hands with as many as he could reach, quite pleased with these expressions of interest.

When we reached the theater some fifteen minutes later, we had the same trouble in gaining the

Valentino as I Knew Him

entrance. As we entered, we could hear the shouts of the audience attempting to silence the announcer, who was vainly endeavoring to quiet their impatience by telling them that Valentino was on the way.

Very quietly Rudy walked on the stage and tapped the announcer on the shoulder. The latter turned with a start.

The great audience was so instantly silenced that you could have heard a pin drop. Then a roar of welcoming applause burst forth which lasted at least three minutes.

It gives me the greatest satisfaction to recall that picture of Rudolph Valentino, as he stood before that vast audience, radiant with health and happiness, smiling boyishly at the sincerity of his welcome. If I had known that death stalked so near, I could not have wished for him any greater joy than came to him during his last five public appearances at the showing of *The Son of the Sheik*. It proved to me, beyond any doubt, that Valentino was indeed the outstanding idol of the screen.

Again he made one of his delightful impromptu speeches, thanking the audience for its appreciation of his efforts and impressing them and me anew with his charm and dignity. At the risk of being considered a bore I repeat that, had Valentino been making a request for contributions for a worthy

"Uncle Rudy" with the author's two children, Ro
Warren and Daniel Bruce, with whom he was a fav

by S. George Ullman

philanthropy, it is my opinion that he could have turned people's pockets wrong side out.

Thence we made our way through the crowds to the broadcasting station on the Steel Pier. While we were waiting for Rudy's scheduled time for going on the air, the crowd surged around, climbing on each other's shoulders and almost breaking the windows in their attempt to see the star.

If the fan letters which poured in to the station after this speech of Rudy's are any criterion, he must have been as much of a success on the air as ever he was on the screen.

Back at the hotel later, Rudy kept his promise of going to Gus Edwards' Revue. Just as we were entering I saw him rush up to a man, seize him by both hands and pour forth a torrent of voluble Italian, to which the other responded with equal excitement.

I asked what the trouble was, fearing the worst, but Rudy reassured me saying that he was not quarreling. That this was a man whom he had asked for a job as bus boy at the Ritz-Carlton in New York when he first came to America, but was refused because the man thought he would be no good.

Gus Edwards seized upon Rudy and introduced him to the audience. He said that, having heard of the bout with Buck O'Neil, he took pleasure

Valentino as I Knew Him

in this publicly presenting him with a pair of boxing gloves. He complimented Rudy upon his fistic ability, of which he had seen examples, and suggested that Rudy use these gloves on the Chicago editor.

Later in the evening, Edwards asked Valentino if he would dance the tango with the professional dancer in his revue. At first Rudy demurred, but finally consented, and danced the tango that he made famous in *The Four Horsemen*.

This was the last time Valentino ever danced the tango.

Chapter 15

Back to New York and a hot drive.

In the ensuing two weeks Rudy had nothing to do except make one public appearance, at the Strand Theater in Brooklyn.

Here the same scenes were enacted. The same heat. The same crowds. The only difference was that in his speech, which he made slightly longer than usual, he paid a fine tribute to Agnes Ayres for the high quality of her sportsmanship in accepting so small a part in *The Son of the Shiek,* since by doing so she had established an important sequence which greatly added to the success of the picture. He also spoke of her in a different rôle, that of wife and mother, picturing her in her charming Hollywood home and referring to her as the mother of a lovely baby. He spoke with so much tenderness of this home picture of the famous movie star as a mother, and described the baby in words of such sincerity that the audience was touched almost to tears, and again there shone in his eyes that indescribable expression which came into them only when he was speaking of children.

Valentino as I Knew Him

Rudy had promised the Stanley Company to make a personal appearance at their Philadelphia theater, where *The Son of the Sheik* was to be shown, and, although he was by this time getting just a little restive under inaction and anxious to get back to work, he would not break his word. Thus he filled in his time in New York between August second and the sixteenth, which was his Philadelphia date. Only death prevented him from keeping this promise.

On the Saturday evening before his final collapse I noticed that his color was bad, and urged him to come home early and get some rest.

As if summoning all his strength, with fire again in his eyes, he said:

"Why, I feel wonderful! I don't need rest!"

I could not help a feeling of anxiety which remained with me all night. Rudy's color was usually so marvelous that any change in it could not fail to attract my attention.

At the first groan from him the next morning I was at his side, and one look at him was enough. Immediately I summoned physicians who, after a hurried consultation, rushed him to Polyclinic Hospital, where he was operated on at six o'clock that evening.

At seven the operation was over, and at ten

by S. George Ullman

thirty he came out from under the influence of the ether.

I want to call the attention of the entire world to the first statement Valentino made when he was conscious.

"Well," he said, "did I behave like a pink powder puff or like a man?"

Which goes to prove my contention that the editorial in *The Chicago Tribune* had a distinct bearing on Rudy's life. And if, in future, editors wishing to cast slurs on those with whom they have no personal acquaintance should be restrained by this unfortunate occurrence, Valentino's suffering will not have been in vain.

At first no one, not even the surgeons who operated, the physicians in attendance, or the nurses, had any doubt as to the outcome. We all thought that Rudy would recover. And when telegrams from all over the country began to pour in expressing anxiety, our first impulse was to reassure his friends and to communicate our hopefulness by means of the public press.

I once expressed to him the fervent wish that I might be suffering in his place, leaving him to go on with his work without interruption, and his reply was:

"Don't be silly! You have a wife and little

Valentino as I Knew Him

children, family responsibilities, whereas I . . ." And he turned his face to the wall.

Later I asked him whether I should send for his brother, to which he replied:

"By no means. Just cable him that I am a little indisposed and will soon be all right. And wire Pola the same."

These almost deathbed statements of my friend are so sacred to me that I would not willingly distort them by so much as a misplaced word, and I quote only those which are necessary to this narrative.

He asked for no one and slept almost all the time. He felt no pain and only expressed himself as being "so tired."

By physicians' orders, no one was allowed to see him nor even to go near his room, for the purpose of enforcing which, I stationed a detective at his door to see that even nurses not on his case could not gain admittance. Notwithstanding the broadcasting of these orders, people continuously tried, by every known ruse, to gain admittance to the hospital and even to storm the corridor in which Valentino was fighting for his life.

Telegrams now began to arrive in such numbers that I was obliged to summon my secretary to handle them. To say that flowers arrived by the truck-load is not to exaggerate.

by S. George Ullman

When he was able to bear a little conversation, I told Rudy about the telegrams and flowers, as well as the special delivery letters and notes sent by hand or by messenger, and explained to him that, owing to the necessity of keeping the air in his room pure, he could only have a few flowers in his room at a time.

Without waiting for me to suggest it, he told me to see that the free wards in the hospital were supplied with his flowers every day.

It was typical of Valentino that he invariably wished to share whatever happiness he had with others.

One day he surprised me by asking for a mirror. I was loath to humor him, as his illness had left marks upon his face I did not wish him to see. He seemed to read my thoughts, for he said:

"Oh, let me have it! I just want to see how I look when I am sick, so that if I ever have to play the part in pictures I will know how to put on my make-up!"

Thus he, too, had no premonition of the short time he had to live.

He was certainly on the road to recovery and, as late as Saturday morning at one-thirty, when Mrs. Ullman and I left him, no one had expressed any anxiety as to the outcome.

Valentino as I Knew Him

Nevertheless I was uneasy. I do not say that I had a premonition. I only know that after I had taken Mrs. Ullman to the hotel and bathed, instead of going to bed I dressed myself again and went back to the hospital, arriving there before five o'clock in the morning.

It was still dark, and the night shift of nurses was still on. Rudy was asleep; but I got his chart from the night nurse and saw, to my consternation, that both his pulse and respiration had increased. Whereupon I immediately telephoned the four physicians to come at once, which they did.

A little before seven Rudy wakened, smiled at me and said:

"I feel fine now. The pain is all gone and I can feel the place where they made the incision. By Monday I think we can have Joe and Norma in, and by Wednesday I will go back to the hotel, taking the nurses, of course."

The doctors then made a thorough examination, and afterwards held a consultation lasting almost an hour. There was the most complete discussion of the symptoms, in which they frankly stated that the sudden cessation of pain was an exceedingly bad sign.

I was by this time so much alarmed that I asked the doctors to cancel all other engagements, put substitutes on their cases and never to be beyond

by S. George Ullman

call, as the case of Valentino was too important for us to run even the slightest risk.

From this time on, Rudy waged courageously his failing fight with death.

Unwilling to leave any stone unturned, I called in another specialist, in the hope that he might have new ideas or be able to suggest something which had not occurred to the others. Every possible method was discussed, even to blood transfusion, but all were discarded one after another as being impracticable.

That night no one slept, and a dreadful air of suspense hung over the entire hospital. The doctors were again forced to issue bulletins and in silence crowds slowly began to gather in the streets, eager for the word of hope which never came.

Early Sunday morning I went again to his bedside and even my unpracticed eyes saw that he was sinking rapidly. His fever had increased, and his pulse was more rapid.

Realizing that were he able to think clearly he would probably wish to see a confessor, I sent for Father Leonard, who had frequently called up during his illness to ask how he was.

The priest came at my summons and was alone with the dying man for some time. When he came out his face was uplifted and I saw that the interview had been satisfactory. Later when I saw

Valentino as I Knew Him

that Rudy was calmer, I felt that I had done right.

Knowing that what was to be done must be done quickly, I telephoned to Mr. Schenck and his wife Norma Talmadge, who were visiting Adolph Zukor at his home in New York City. Also to Frank Mennillo, one of Rudy's dearest Italian friends.

About half past four, Mr. and Mrs. Schenck arrived and Norma waited in another room while I took Mr. Schenck into the sick room.

At first we thought Rudy was asleep; but, sensing our presence, he opened his eyes and said, in a weak voice:

"Mighty nice of you to come to see me. How is Norma? How is Connie?"

Totally unable to control his feelings despite his best efforts, Mr. Schenck stood there, holding Rudy's hand, tears running down his cheeks. Finally he pulled himself together enough to say:

"Everybody's fine! And—and you must get well, too!"

Rudy forced a smile so wan that it belied his brave words, and said:

"I'll be all right."

Nothing more was said, and we went out to where Norma was anxiously waiting, so deeply moved that she was almost on the verge of a collapse.

by S. George Ullman

Early in the evening Frank Mennillo arrived, and, after I broke the news to him of Rudy's serious condition, we went in and he spoke to Rudy in Italian. But Rudy answered, in English:

"Thank you, Frank. I'm going to be well soon."

All during the night the doctors, Frank Mennillo and I kept watch. I went into Rudy's room at least every hour, but found that he was sleeping quietly, until about four o'clock Monday morning, when I observed that he was tossing about and in great pain.

At once I called the doctors, who came hurriedly and did everything they could to relieve him.

About six o'clock, when I was again in the room, Rudy recognized me and called me by name in a voice so much stronger that I felt encouraged, until he went on to say:

"Wasn't it an awful thing that we were lost in the woods last night?"

Too shocked to reply, I simply stroked his hair. He looked up at me and said:

"On the one hand you don't appreciate the humor of that. Do you?"

I tried to smile and said:

"Sure I do, Rudy. Sure I do."

Valentino as I Knew Him

A quizzical look came into his eyes and he said again:

"On the other hand, you don't seem to appreciate the seriousness of it either."

Fearing to excite him further, I turned away and, hoping that he would drop off to sleep, I went to the window to pull down the blinds, since the sun was just rising and the room was growing light.

I turned at the sound of his voice. He waved a feeble hand and, with a wistful smile just touching his lips, he said:

"Don't pull down the blinds! I feel fine. I want the sunlight to greet me."

I turned with a start, for I could not fail to sense that the light he referred to was that of another world.

These were the last intelligible words he ever spoke.

Hurriedly I summoned an Italian priest, thinking that possibly Rudy might wish to say something in his native tongue to a confessor, but when he arrived Rudy was too far gone to answer, and only muttered one Italian word, which no one could understand.

So died Rudolph Valentino. Gallantly, as he had lived.

THE END

The greatest pleasure in life is that of reading. Why not then own the books of great novelists when the price is so small

¶ Of all the amusements which can possibly be imagined for a hard-working man, after his daily toil, or in its intervals, there is nothing like reading an entertaining book. It calls for no bodily exertion. It transports him into a livelier, and gayer, and more diversified and interesting scene, and while he enjoys himself there he may forget the evils of the present moment. Nay, it accompanies him to his next day's work, and gives him something to think of besides the mere mechanical drudgery of his every-day occupation—something he can enjoy while absent, and look forward with pleasure to return to.

Ask your dealer for a list of the titles in Burt's Popular Priced Fiction

In buying the books bearing the A. L. Burt Company imprint you are assured of wholesome, entertaining and instructive reading

THE BEST OF RECENT FICTION

Crimson Tide, The. Robert W. Chambers.
Cross Currents. Author of "Pollyanna."
Cross Pull, The. Hal G. Evarts.
Cry in the Wilderness, A. Mary E. Waller.
Cry of Youth, A. Cynthia Lombardi.
Cup of Fury, The. Rupert Hughes.
Curious Quest, The. E. Phillips Oppenheim.
Curved Blades, The. Carolyn Wells.
Cytherea. Joseph Hergesheimer.

Damsel in Distress, A. Pelham G. Wodehouse.
Dancing Star, The. Berta Ruck.
Danger and Other Stories. A. Conan Doyle.
Dark Hollow. Anna Katharine Green.
Daughter Pays, The. Mrs. Baillie Reynolds.
Depot Master, The. Joseph C. Lincoln.
Desert Healer, The. E. M. Hull.
Destroying Angel, The. Louis Joseph Vance. (Photoplay Ed.).
Devil's Paw, The. E. Phillips Oppenheim.
Diamond Thieves, The. Arthur Stringer.
Disturbing Charm, The. Berta Ruck.
Donnegan. George Owen Baxter.
Door of Dread, The. Arthur Stringer.
Doors of the Night. Frank L. Packard.
Dope. Sax Rohmer.
Double Traitor, The. E. Phillips Oppenheim.
Dust of the Desert. Robert Welles Ritchie.

Empty Hands. Arthur Stringer.
Empty Pockets. Rupert Hughes.
Empty Sack, The. Basil King.
Enchanted Canyon. Honoré Willsie.
Enemies of Women. V. B. Ibanez. (Photoplay Ed.).
Eris. Robert W. Chambers.
Erskine Dale, Pioneer. John Fox, Jr.
Evil Shepherd, The. E. Phillips Oppenheim.
Extricating Obadiah. Joseph C. Lincoln.
Eye of Zeitoon, The. Talbot Mundy.
Eyes of the Blind. Arthur Somers Roche.
Eyes of the World. Harold Bell Wright.

Fair Harbor. Joseph C. Lincoln.
Family. Wayland Wells Williams.
Fathoms Deep. Elizabeth Stancy Payne.
Feast of the Lanterns. Louise Gordon Miln.
Fighting Chance, The. Robert W. Chambers.

AT A POPULAR PRICE

Fighting Shepherdess, The. Caroline Lockhart.
Financier, The. Theodore Dreiser.
Fire Tongue. Sax Rohmer.
Flaming Jewel, The. Robert W. Chambers.
Flowing Gold. Rex Beach.
Forbidden Trail, The. Honoré Willsie.
Forfeit, The. Ridgwell Cullum.
Four Million, The. O. Henry.
Foursquare. Grace S. Richmond.
Four Stragglers, The. Frank L. Packard.
Free Range Lanning. George Owen Baxter.
From Now On. Frank L. Packard.
Fur Bringers, The. Hulbert Footner.
Further Adventures of Jimmie Dale. Frank L. Packard.
Galusha the Magnificent. Joseph C. Lincoln.
Gaspards of Pine Croft, The. Ralph Connor.
Gay Year, The. Dorothy Speare.
Gift of the Desert. Randall Parrish.
Girl in the Mirror, The. Elizabeth Jordan.
Girl from Kellers, The. Harold Bindloss.
Girl Philippa, The. Robert W. Chambers.
Girls at His Billet, The. Berta Ruck.
Glory Rides the Range. Ethel and James Dorrance.
God's Country and the Woman. James Oliver Curwood.
God's Good Man. Marie Correlli.
Going Some. Rex Beach.
Gold Girl, The. James B. Hendryx.
Gold-Killer. John Prosper.
Golden Scorpion, The. Sax Rohmer.
Golden Slipper, The. Anna Katherine Green.
Golden Woman, The. Ridgwell Cullum.
Gray Phantom, The. Herman Landon.
Gray Phantom's Return, The. Herman Landon.
Great Impersonation, The. E. Phillips Oppenheim.
Great Prince Shan, The. E. Phillips Oppenheim.
Greater Love Hath No Man. Frank L. Packard.
Green Eyes of Bast, The. Sax Rohmer.
Green Goddess, The. Louise Jordan Miln. (Photoplay Ed.).
Greyfriars Bobby. Eleanor Atkinson.
Gun Brand, The. James B. Hendryx.
Gun Runner, The. Arthur Stringer.
Guns of the Gods. Talbot Mundy.
Hand of Fu-Manchu, The. Sax Rohmer.
Hand of Peril, The. Arthur Stringer.

THE BEST OF RECENT FICTION

Harbor Road, The. Sara Ware Bassett.
Harriet and the Piper. Kathleen Norris.
Havoc. E. Phillips Oppenheim.
Head of the House of Coombe, The. Frances Hodgson Burnett.
Heart of the Desert, The. Honoré Willsie.
Heart of the Hills, The. John Fox, Jr.
Heart of the Range, The. William Patterson White.
Heart of the Sunset. Rex Beach.
Heart of Unaga, The. Ridgwell Cullum.
Helen of the Old House. Harold Bell Wright.
Hidden Places, The. Bertrand W. Sinclair.
Hidden Trails. William Patterson White.
Hillman, The. E. Phillips Oppenheim.
Hira Singh. Talbot Mundy.
His Last Bow. A. Conan Doyle.
His Official Fiancee. Berta Ruck.
Homeland. Margaret Hill McCarter.
Homestead Ranch. Elizabeth G. Young.
Honor of the Big Snows. James Oliver Curwood.
Hopalong Cassidy. Clarence E. Mulford.
Hound from the North, The. Ridgwell Cullum.
House of the Whispering Pines, The. Anna Katharine Green
Humoresque. Fannie Hurst.
Illustrious Prince, The. E. Phillips Oppenheim.
In Another Girl's Shoes. Berta Ruck.
Indifference of Juliet, The. Grace S. Richmond.
Infelice. Augusta Evans Wilson.
Initials Only. Anna Katharine Green.
Innocent. Marie Corelli.
Innocent Adventuress, The. Mary Hastings Bradley.
Insidious Dr. Fu-Manchu, The. Sax Rohmer.
In the Brooding Wild. Ridgwell Cullum.
In the Onyx Lobby. Carolyn Wells.
Iron Trail, The. Rex Beach.
Iron Woman, The. Margaret Deland.
Ishmael. (Ill.) Mrs. Southworth.
Isle of Retribution. Edison Marshall.
I've Married Marjorie. Margaret Widdemer.
Ivory Trail, The. Talbot Mundy.
Jacob's Ladder. E. Phillips Oppenheim.
Jean of the Lazy A. B. M. Bower.
Jeanne of the Marshes. E. Phillips Oppenheim.
Jeeves. P. G. Wodehouse.